YOU ARE YOUR OWN

*A Reckoning
with the Religious Trauma
of Evangelical Christianity*

Jamie Lee Finch

JamieLeeFinch.com.

Cover photo by Bree Marie Fish (BreeMarieFish.com). Cover layout by Caitlin Metz and Tucker FitzGerald. Book layout by Tucker FitzGerald (TuckerLFitzGerald.com)

All hand lettering by Caitlin Metz (www.CaitlinMetzArt.com).

Back cover headshot by Ashtin Paige (AshtinPaige.com)

ISBN 9781075246302

Set in Utopia.

To Twitter

CONTENTS

INTRODUCTION

This work consists of a brief overview of the history of Evangelical Christianity in the United States that is rarely told to young believers brought up in the religion. My personal narrative—my experiences of growing up in Evangelical Christianity, and its damaging effects—grounds what follows. Drawing on scholarly research, I explain how the cumulative effects of the psychologically problematic elements of these beliefs so often lead to the "religious trauma syndrome" identified in people raised with them (Winell). Finally, this work includes insight into and recommendations for recovery and rebuilding for survivors who have left the extremist belief systems they were raised in. Inspired by my own experience as a former devout Evangelical believer, this work is the beginning of the larger, life-long work I will continue not only for the sake of others but also for myself—to share my story after 20 years of not being able to tell the truth.

When I first arrived at Goddard to study, a faculty member advised us as new students to pay less attention to the conversations we were having with our advisors in our study groups, and more attention to the conversations we were finding ourselves engaging in around the dinner table. They encouraged us to take notice of what we were saying whenever people would lean in and ask us to tell them more, and informed us that those moments were the indicators of what we were actually here to study. So I began to pay attention; and what I noticed was that whenever I was talking about my own former experience with religious devotion, it became quickly apparent that people were leaning in. Throughout most of my life, I have spanned the spectrum of Evangelicalism, even moving to a different country to join (what I obviously didn't know at the time was) a cult. And during those dinner time discussions, I not only found a solidarity with so many people explaining that was their background too, but witnessed a newly ignited passion in so many of them as they would respond with "I hadn't thought of it that way before" or "this makes me feel less crazy and alone".

Now, holding space for the recovery from this exact background is what I do for a living as an embodiment coach who specializes in helping people heal from religious trauma and sexual suppression. What lies ahead in these pages is equal parts academic study and lived experience. While I do not tell any specific, confidential client stories here, the recognition and explanation of the anxieties, imbalances, and dysfunctions due to the trauma of this religious devotion that they share with me daily are all over these pages. Additionally, I recognize the limitations present in this work rooted in the pain of my personal experience, anger I often feel at the institution on behalf of my clients and loved ones, and the time constraints of only a year and a half of study and writing. I was unable to go as in depth into specific traumatizing doctrines as well as the brain science of trauma as I would have liked, and I recognize that because of this there are many people for whom this work may not resonate. Nevertheless, it exists for the millions of people who share my own experience and language, and my limitations do not invalidate the fact that this particular trauma is present in our minds and bodies. It is my hope that this work will serve to validate and comfort survivors, as well as educate those either still within Christian practices or those who have never been familiar with belief at all.

HISTORY and OVERVIEW

"Do you not know that your bodies are temples of the Holy Spirit, who is in you, whom you have received from God? You are not your own; you were bought at a price. Therefore honor God with your bodies."

1 Corinthians 6:19-20 NIV

It's inevitable, predictable, one of the few things I've grown to be able to count on these days. For the past few years of academic work and building my coaching business, it has happened almost the exact same way every time. No matter what part of the country, no matter what situation or context in which we're meeting, no matter what led us to this point in the conversation—upon telling someone what I do for a living or how it informs what I've been writing, I receive one of two reactions.

The first is from folks who are mostly on the outside and have spent the majority of their life there. In light of the 2016 election of Donald J. Trump to the office of the Presidency of the United States, they ask: "How did we get here? Can you explain this to me?" And I tell them that I hate to say that I know exactly what they mean. I receive this inquiry primarily from people who identify as non- or nominally-religious, but occasionally it also comes from individuals who identify somewhere along the spectrum of mainline Protestant Christianity. Regardless, the one thing that they all have in common is that they desire context for what they have seen: that 81% of white Evangelical Christians in America voted for Trump, and that he received the bulk of his support from prominent white Evangelical leaders like Jerry Falwell Jr., Franklin Graham, Rick Joyner, Robert Jeffress, James Dobson, and their followers.

Even as I was first drafting this work in early 2018, the United States was living in the shadow of a series of bombings in Austin, Texas—acts of terror against people of color committed by a white male raised as an Evangelical Christian. The sad reality is, this violence has not been given the proper classification by the media that it deserves, not only because of our nation's embedded bias towards white supremacy, but also because there is not nearly enough cultural competency surrounding the reality of the subcultures that exist within Evangelicalism and the true harm they cause. By and large, the media does not grasp the full scope of the belief system and just how easily and often it bends towards extremism.

But it's only by having been there that anyone could truly see this, and that's why the second reaction I inevitably receive from people after I tell them what I do comes from those who have also left the fold: "I get it. I've been there. Me too." Because we see the sickness so clearly. We know what it taught us about ourselves and what it told us about the way the world works, so we know exactly how our culture and our country "got here"—because it's devastatingly clear to us how long so many have already been here. That specific sickness, however, can often be more easily identified in the public displays of institutional violence and more difficult to notice when it is active inside of the bodies and minds of individual people.

The truth is that religious trauma has consequences; a significant and long-lasting impact on the brain and the body, and I see these effects most prevalent in the belief system that is Evangelical Christianity—particularly for the ones who were raised within it as children. Survivors must have the permission to know and be in touch with the full scope of what has happened to them if they are going to heal. They have to be willing, able, and brave enough to become curious about what happened in their minds during their developmental years and what stories their bodies are telling now.

This work intends to act as a beacon, to release that permission, and to give an accurate name to the often mysterious embodied experience of countless people who are coming out of the belief and practice of Evangelicalism. For so many of my friends and clients alike, when I tell them I believe that what they're experiencing in their psychology and physiology is not only normal in light of their experience, but deserves the term "trauma", the relief is palpable. As Dr. Wendell Watters points out in his attempt to frame a similar hypothesis in his work *Deadly Doctrine*, mental health professionals often include the religious background in their case reports for their patients, "but the possibility that the patient's experiences with religion could have had some role to play in the production of symptoms is never entertained" (Watters 21). This work intends to bridge that gap and offer language that will enable survivors of Evangelical Christianity's authoritarian propaganda to embark on their own healing.

In order to contextualize my experiences of growing up in this belief system, I begin by locating my specific focus on Evangelical Christianity within the larger context of Christianity that exists in varying forms and expressions throughout the world. To do this, it is important for me to clarify what I mean and what I do not mean; who I am referring to and who I am not referring to when I use the term Evangelicalism or Evangelical Christianity. A few of the distinguishing characteristics of Evangelical Christians in the Western world are belief in the historical accuracy and literal interpretation of both the Hebrew Bible and the New Testament, particularly the divinity, death, and resurrection of Jesus the Christ, and belief in the necessity of personal conversion—being "born again"—as a condition for salvation. Additionally, Evangelical Christians believe that conversion and salvation are necessary because of the existence of a place of eternal conscious torment called Hell that all people in their natural state are deserving of—because they have been born into a nature of inherited sin.

Evangelicalism arrived at its particular position in the 21st century by way of fundamentalist development in the twentieth. As Chris Ladd, a former conservative, writes, "Evangelicalism today has been co-opted as a preferred description for Christians who were looking to shed an older, largely discredited title: Fundamentalist" (Ladd "Why White Evangelicalism"). Though this is not the place for detailed debate over the 19th and 20th century transformation of Evangelicalism, it is worth mentioning the slightly nuanced view of developments in Northern Evangelicalism offered in Evangelical Michael Gerson's sad discussion of the roots of contemporary beliefs and practices.

In the years before the Civil War, a connection between moralism and a concern for social justice was generally assumed among Northern Evangelicals. They variously advocated for temperance, humane treatment of the mentally disabled, and prison reform. But mainly they militated for the end of slavery. Indeed, Wheaton [College founded in 1860 by abolitionist Evangelicals] welcomed both African American and female students, and served as a stop on the Underground Railroad ("The Last Temptation").

Gerson sees a huge shift in values from the mid-19th century when Evangelicalism was the main religious tradition in America and "welcoming of progress" to its present contradictory support of Donald Trump's worst unchristian excesses. He claims that progressive Evangelicals initially sought "common ground" between faith, new criticism, and science.

Many combined their faith with the Social Gospel—a postmillennialism drained of the miraculous, with social reform taking the place of the Second Coming. Religious conservatives, by contrast, rebelled against this strategy of accommodation in a series of firings and heresy trials designed to maintain control of seminaries. (Woodrow Wilson's uncle James lost his job at Columbia Theological Seminary for accepting evolution as compatible with the Bible.) But these tactics generally backfired, and seminary after seminary, college after college, fell under the influence of modern scientific and cultural assumptions. To contest progressive ideas, the religiously orthodox published a series of books called *The Fundamentals*. Hence the term *fundamentalism*, conceived in a spirit of desperate reaction.

This was not a return to earlier forms of Evangelical belief, but a reaction against contemporary criticism that questioned the Bible's historicity and so instead:

...it became simplistic and overliteral in its reading of scripture. In reacting against evolution, it became anti-scientific in its general orientation. In reacting against the Social Gospel, it came to regard the whole concept of social justice as a dangerous liberal idea. This last point constituted what some scholars have called the "Great Reversal," which took place from about 1900 to 1930 (Gerson "The Last Temptation").

In recent decades white Evangelicalism has greatly influenced political conservatism and the development of the Religious Right during the latter half of the 20th century (Fitzgerald 9). Its political identification with conservatism helps to expose some of the idiosyncrasies of the modern Evangelical experience and it is crucial to note that partnership. Many of us who now consider ourselves "Exvangelical" were children during the height of the prolonged political, social, and religious moment between the late 1970s on through the early 2000s; metaphorically bookmarked by the presidential elections of Ronald Reagan and George W. Bush. To see Evangelical Christianity for what it is clearly, we have to acknowledge its obsession with obtaining and securing a position of dominant political power.

When speaking of Evangelicalism it is important to point out that the term, while often encompassing many denominations, is predominantly invoked when speaking of the Southern Baptist denomination—a group with an extremely problematic history because its commitment to maintaining white supremacy played a role in its growth and development. Just before the Civil War, southern churches were under incredible pressure from white plantation owners to distance themselves from the growing narratives of social and political justice surrounding abolition (Ladd, "Why White Evangelicalism"). On this point, Chris Ladd writes:

> *Generation after generation, Southern pastors adapted their theology to thrive under a terrorist state. Principled critics were exiled or murdered, leaving voices of dissent few and scattered. Southern Christianity evolved in strange directions under ever-increasing isolation. Preachers learned to tailor their message to protect themselves. If all you knew about Christianity came from a close reading of the New Testament, you'd expect that Christians would be hostile to wealth, emphatic in protection of justice, sympathetic to the point of personal pain toward the sick, persecuted and the migrant, and almost socialist in their economic practices. None of these consistent Christian themes served the interests of slave owners, so pastors could either abandon them, obscure them, or flee* ("Why White Evangelicalism").

Ladd goes on to explain that the primary stronghold of Evangelicalism in the world today is centered in the southern United States where the Southern Baptist denomination, the second largest Christian denomination after Catholicism, remains "the leader in membership, theological pull, and political influence" ("Why White Evangelicalism"). More than one hundred and fifty years after the end of the Civil War and after half a century of our nation living in the wake of the Civil Rights Movement, America's most powerful Evangelical denomination "remains defined, right down to the name over the door, by an 1845 split over slavery" ("Why White Evangelicalism").

This was both the political and religious paradigm of my childhood, the container in which my primary formative years of neurological and behavioral development occurred. The denomination and expression into which I was born and raised was Southern Baptist, and though I made my way through various other denominations later on throughout my early adulthood, the Southern Baptist theological teachings were my first belief imprint. Being Southern Baptist was an extremely defining part of my life and family growing up—in fact, I cannot think of any other primary identifying factor or way of defining who I was and who we were as a family.

Our specific Evangelical belief influenced everything: the way I thought of and about myself, engaged my imagination, made friends, spent time both alone and with family, the media I consumed, and the language I spoke. Eventually, it also steered my educational and life choices as I was taken out of public school after elementary school and sent instead to a private non-accredited

Christian school my parents struggled to afford simply because they feared I would be too influenced by secular culture. My parents claimed that they intended me to receive a better education when in reality, the education offered to me was far worse than that of the public schools in my district. I know now, years later, that their decision was exclusively religiously and racially motivated as the public school district I had previously attended started integrating with students from a failing "inner city" school the very same year I was pulled out.

I would eventually delay my own further education altogether and forgo college in favor of ministry work and missionary travel because education was not nearly as important as doing the lord's work and accomplishing god's mission laid out for us by our Evangelical beliefs— saving lost souls as quickly as possible before their death or the return of Jesus at the unknown but divinely-appointed time of the apocalypse. Evangelical Christianity was integrated into every single part of my life, and I was as involved and as engaged as I could possibly be—or, at least as far as was possible for a female in the system deeply rooted in sexism and a commitment to complementarian-style beliefs. While I did jump into and out of different Evangelical denominations in my twenty years of worship and service, the central themes and foundational beliefs among which I struggled in vain to flourish were the same. It would be many years before I would discover their deep and lasting impact.

It may sound strange, but very little of what you'll find in this work involves the actual Bible, or even the historical figure of Jesus; that is not an oversight. I'm here to speak to a specific religious representation that has developed over the last few decades, and what has come from the gradual distillation of those teachings into the main areas of belief that are most commonly communicated as the central themes of what has emerged as Evangelicalism—the religion that cannot be found in the Bible and that Jesus never intended to create. True to my experience and the experience of many other survivors I speak to and work with, there are many problematic doctrines to choose from and to investigate more closely.

Many of the harmful beliefs and teachings here are not shared by all mainline Protestant groups, but they are consistent to the core values of most Evangelical Christian churches at large. And the pervasive danger of that reality is what Wendell Watters writes in his work *Deadly Doctrine*—that these beliefs have infiltrated the larger arena of Western society as a whole. We need to be concerned about the impact of Evangelical doctrine on individuals in society, as that doctrine acts through the family, educational system, and churches (22). Additionally, in accordance with the Evangelical obsession with political power, Watters points out that "these doctrinal messages are woven into the fabric of society and encoded in secular legislation such as laws regarding sexuality and reproduction" (22). We see this displayed clearly in the words of Jerry Falwell in 1989 when he stated that, "Our goal has been achieved. The religious right is solidly in place and religious conservative values in American are now in for the duration" (Moral Majority. 2018, September 14).

While the belief in the inerrancy of scripture is problematic at best and often the focus of debate, such discussion is beyond the goals of this work. Whether or not inerrancy is reasonable, I contend that those who subscribe to Evangelical beliefs have already accepted the inerrancy and literalism of their scripture. Many Evangelical churches now have identifying statements of faith on their websites, such as this one that speaks directly to the belief in biblical inerrancy: "We believe that God has spoken in the Scriptures, both Old and New Testaments, through the words of human authors. As the verbally inspired Word of God, *the Bible is without error* in the original writings the complete revelation for His will for salvation and the ultimate authority by which every realm of human knowledge and endeavor should be judged. Therefore, it is to be believed in all that it teaches, obeyed in all that it requires, and trusted in all that it promises ("Our Denomination"; my emphasis).

Ultimately, even though a considerable number of Americans identify as Evangelical Christians, what that term communicates about a person, community, or system can be difficult to understand. As Frances Fitzgerald sums up in the introduction to her work *The Evangelicals*:

Many equate Evangelicals with fundamentalists or the Christian right when only a minority belong to either group. Others dismiss them as a marginal group doomed to extinction with the process of modernization. In fact, Evangelicals compose nearly a quarter of the population. They are also the most American of religious groups, and during the nineteenth century they exerted a dominant influence on American culture, morals, and politics. By the mid-twentieth century the United States was becoming a more sexual nation, but since 1980 many Evangelicals, led by the Christian right, have struggled to reverse the trend, and while they have not entirely succeeded, they have reintroduced religion into public discourse, polarized the nation, and profoundly changed American politics (Fitzgerald 2).

In truth, Evangelicalism has undergone many growths, shifts, and changes over the years, but just as fundamentalism reacted against the progress of culture, the white Evangelicalism I was born into was no different. Our family's commitment to this belief system came from my father's side—my mother converted in her late 20s after separation from her first husband prior to meeting my father. My dad was raised Southern Baptist in Texas in a family that was deeply influenced by the ministry and figure of Billy Graham. None of his grandparents were exceptionally religious and both of his parents were either orphaned or separated from their biological families by the age of 12. It's possible their personal experiences with instability made the promise of familial stability offered in white Evangelicalism that much more appealing to them; regardless, theirs was a gospel most rooted in correct social, political, and personal behavior.

By the 1950s, Evangelical belief had become arguably less rooted in the teachings of the Rabbi Jesus and more concentrated in maintaining a morality measured by upholding societal decorum and traditional gender roles. The Christian life that leaders like Graham described was largely concerned with domestic life and the proper execution of the roles of men and women as husbands and wives within the nuclear family (Fitzgerald 196). They advocated that the foremost concern for good Christians was to live disciplined lives in full submission to authority (Fitzgerald 196).

The sexual and political revolutions of the 60s and 70s led to a further reactionary rise of fundamentalism primarily in the southern United States, and more moderate voiced Evangelical leaders such as Graham began to lose their influence (Fitzgerald 7). Pastors and televangelists like Jerry Falwell and Pat Robertson seized the opportunity to enter the arena of national politics, forming groups and organizations such as the Moral Majority, the Christian Voice, and the Religious Roundtable (Fitzgerald 7). These leaders vehemently opposed what they targeted as the "evils" of society—racially integrated schools, comprehensive sex education, abortion, homosexuality, and the influence of big government (Fitzgerald 7). They clung to nationalism and a deeply rooted belief in America having previously been a "Christian nation", but that term was employed uncomfortably often in response to the increase in racial equality in the United States.

What lit the fire in many of these leaders to establish religious and politically conservative strongholds and begin the so called "culture wars" was their indignation over the federal government's attempt to desegregate Evangelical colleges (Fitzgerald 304). The threat of the removal of the tax-exempt status of Christian schools that refused to desegregate infuriated the most powerful Evangelical leaders, causing them to raise their voices to warn families of the societal ills of public education and in effect, the entire secular world. James Dobson, easily the largest and most influential Evangelical voice of my childhood, used his radio show and newsletter to warn of the threat that our changing culture presented to Christian families (Fitzgerald 303). His influence was vast and powerful. Jessica Wilbanks writes her memories of his pamphlets reaching all the way to rural Maryland in the early 90's in her memoir, *When I Spoke in Tongues*:

The little I knew about sex came from the thick letters my parents received every week, mass-mailed from Colorado Springs and bearing the signature of Dr. James Dobson, the head of Focus on the Family. Every week the letters related another travesty—teenage pregnancy, child molesters, gay teachers trying to convert our youth. From those letters, I knew that when two married people had sex, it was fine because the Lord wanted there to be more children in the world. But when sex went wrong—outside of marriage, in unnatural configurations, there was nothing the Lord hated more (Wilbanks, 53).

This reactionary, fear-based language saturated the Evangelical spaces in which I and millions of other Evangelical children developed. Our commission was to separate ourselves from culture in order to remain unaffected, so that we could in turn influence culture and bring it under submission to Christ. So while it's necessary to bring clarity to my story and to state that not every Evangelical experience is identical to mine, these particular male leaders with these voices, beliefs, and impact were in the eyes and ears of millions of Evangelical parents, warning them of the dangers of "secular culture" and the outside world. These leaders built multi-billion dollar corporations, businesses, and empires organized around the intention of equipping Evangelicals for this culture war they must wage in order to win the world for god— and they exerted their influence primarily in the political sphere. As David Gushee writes, "The embrace of Donald Trump in 2016 by most white Evangelicals was just the latest sign either of the bankruptcy of Evangelicals or the meaninglessness of the category. To the extent there is a real thing called American Evangelicalism, it is deeply damaged by now" (Gushee 146).

This deeply damaged iteration of Evangelical belief that Gushee names is entrenched in the language of the binary—everything is either right or wrong, black or white, and there is little tolerance for nuance or the recognition of personal preference and agency. Obviously this spirit isn't exclusive to white Evangelical Christianity, as there are many other extremist belief systems around the world that function similarly. But this is my experience and the experience of millions of others in this particular belief and branch of belief. While my experience is not the exclusive experience inside of Evangelical Christianity, it most certainly is not unique. The consequences are vast and we are beginning to see a rise in these stories—in television news specials, podcasts, and memoirs all covering the phenomenon of Evangelical religious deconstruction and reconstruction.

What I have also come to realize through this research and study is that the history of Evangelical influence that I was previously taught was mired in more mythology than truth; the successes, the reach, the impact upon the world was never quite as vast or as singularly celebratory as many leaders had claimed (Fitzgerald 317). As with most things, the truth is much more nuanced. And in light of the fact that there are many people who no longer identify as Evangelical but still identify as Christian, many who no longer identify as either, and many who still cling to both, I am learning to leave room for the nuance that welcomes and validates the experience of everyone along that spectrum. Additionally, I acknowledge the blind spots present in my own view due to the pain of my experience and the pain I hear daily in the voices of my clients, podcast listeners, followers on social media, and friends. The truth is that there have long been Evangelical voices crying in the wilderness, denouncing what they have seen and experienced as problematic and harmful within the institution—particularly in the moments when it has married itself to political power.

Throughout my study, I have discovered that though the spirit of prophetic dissent has been there all along, it has long been controlled and censored out of the presiding narrative (Fitzgerald 544). I write this work from that same spirit; my dissent, however, focuses less on issues of social justice and more on psychological and developmental impact. Some of my closest friends remain devout in their Christian practice, and most of my family remains identified as Evangelical. I am not here to swing over to the opposite side of a fundamentalist viewpoint—I am here to bring as much clarity from a psychological and behavioral perspective as possible. There is freedom for people to identify with and choose whatever belief they decide is best for them, but it is imperative that we begin honestly discussing the consequences of many of the beliefs upheld within Evangelical Christianity. In many ways, the impact of the institution is unknown even to itself and I deeply want to believe that if those with the greatest influence truly knew, they would be willing to shift away from beliefs that harm to beliefs that heal.

This work focuses on those harmful beliefs and not only the problems they directly cause, but the more nuanced issues that grow from their acceptance on both personal and societal levels, particularly when implanted in the developing minds of vulnerable children. Many Evangelicals who subscribe to this system methodically indoctrinate their children into believing in phenomena like "the rapture", the value of redemptive violence, the existence of a place of eternal torture after death, an inherited and unavoidable state of sin, the impurity of the female body, and the impossibility of achieving god's love without surrendering to all the system's beliefs. Even when those beliefs—if laid out side by side—are often contradictory.

People who have not experienced this indoctrination would probably say there's nothing methodical—nothing *rational*—at all in the arguments fed to children. While I agree now, the reality is that it took many years for me to gather the courage to begin to step away. Early on, rejecting the belief system in its entirety was not possible— the stakes were far too high as the fear of divine consequence felt far too real. So I methodically sought other systems or churches that could still deliver god but not so frighteningly; that would relieve my fears about what god would do to me, the sinner seeking to assuage her doubts. Instead, I incurred more self-disgust, fear and loathing of my own body in each new environment, and that in turn brought me to deeper patterns of self-destructive behavior. In this study, I offer the "plain facts" of how individuals—particularly children—are abused in this system of belief, and illustrate those facts with excerpts from my own personal writing throughout my formative years alongside other "evidence" of the psychological torture and corporal punishments I received in order to ensure that I would be "saved and sanctified" from my sin and self.

It is my belief that teaching harmful Evangelical religious beliefs to children begets an alarming number of psychological and physical imbalances, as well as behaviorally and socially maladaptive traits. Because of this, it is important to take an honest and candid look at the impact of the teachings of the Evangelical church, establish the ways in which they cause real and valid trauma in the individuals who were socialized to accept them, and offer avenues of recovery for those who have survived and are seeking healing—all while offering my own story as a guide along the way.

My Story

As noted above, I was initially raised Southern Baptist, spent the majority of my adolescence involved in Presbyterian and Non-Denominational churches and schools (the latter, surprisingly, is its own denomination) and had a brief dabble with Catholicism in my late teens. My early 20s were given over to a denomination known as Acts 29 that espouses rigid Calvinism and "reformed" theology, right before I dove head first into Charismatic Pentecostalism prior to my eventual deconstruction and departure from the entire Christian belief narrative altogether.

The Evangelical personal salvation narrative essentially begins with the doctrine of original sin—a belief that stems from Adam and Eve's choice of knowledge over god. To disobey god, in this storyline, is to sin; and god's disappointment and wrath then condemns all born of Adam and Eve (the entire human race) to be born as sinners. Our first parents' decision to stray from god and enact their own will by choosing their own desires separated all people from his presence and permanently altered the state of the world and permanently corrupted humanity, thus permanently dooming both our bodies and souls.

Central to this belief is the assumption that we as humankind are born with a built-in urge to rebel against goodness and morality, and that our depraved state leaves us in desperate need of rescuing from divine wrath. Everything that makes us human—our bodies, our flesh—is instinctively bent towards disobedience and evil. We cannot save ourselves, we cannot trust ourselves, and whatever is in us that is of the flesh and not of the spirit is corrupted by sin. Believing that "all have sinned and fallen short of the glory of god" often makes it difficult to develop positive feelings towards those who do not share this belief—because their failure to believe makes them unworthy of compassion or empathy. The best that may be offered those perceived as "other" is an imperious, infantilizing sympathy; similarly, believers do not often feel permission to extend compassion and empathy towards themselves.

For many who grew up in Evangelical Christianity, the narrative that "self-esteem is evil" tainted our formative years. We were told that only "god esteem" was allowed because our "self"—our true self, our flesh—was so corrupt that it could not be believed nor supported on its own. Therefore, regardless of what we wished to believe our intentions could be, our own motivations and impulses and those of all others had to be regarded as impure and capable of being mobilized by unseen, cosmic forces of evil.

For my part, being told that I was evil at such a young age was dizzying—the problem and the solution were presented to me at the same time in tandem. The mistrust of self and body, of desire and pleasure was planted early. As a young child, I was required to engage with and give account of Bible verses telling me that my own flesh was something to be fought against, resisted, and put to death. And if holy scripture told me that my own flesh was solely something to hate, to vilify, and to blame then the body that it covered—my own body—was someone I could not and should not ever attempt to relate to, understand, or love.

The moment I was made aware that I was required to believe in my inherited depraved state, I instantly had to start believing that my own self was no longer safe and required divine intervention to become safe again. If I didn't adhere to that belief, it meant that I was not repentant enough to understand that I needed salvation; if that was the case, I could not be saved. The pure self-esteem I had as a child abruptly stopped—because it had to—otherwise, I was living in sin. To resist repentance was to believe in myself too much, and to believe in myself too much was to be actively deceived and used by the devil.

If the only good thing about me was outside of me, then nothing in me was good. I sacrificed years to prayers admitting and confirming this guilt over and over. I sent countless confessions up to the ceiling about how if I was left to myself, I would inevitably ruin my own life. I wrote a multitude of journal entries during my most formative years about how bad and dirty I not only was, but was always doomed to be—how I needed god to purify me from my evil desires and empty me of my own self in order to have the life I believed he required of me. I deeply believed that everything I wanted was bad—simply because I wanted it. I wrote poetry and prose from early childhood well into my late 20s about hating myself and how hating myself enough was the only way I could be certain of my salvation; how I was weak for wanting and how I needed the power of god to release me from this power of sin within.

Additionally, as a girl growing into a woman, the specific experience of being told not to trust myself, my body, and how my true nature was corrupted with sin was particularly troubling. In the narrative embodiment work I do with my clients, I share with them something called my "Creation Story"—an excerpt from which speaks to this experience well:

> As I grew and developed, the messages I was receiving from my religion morphed, but a sense of safety never appeared. As I approached adolescence, I became well acquainted with more unsettling messages within my authoritarian Evangelicalism: namely, that my female body was the root of evil and had even caused the initial "fall of man" in the first place. Apparently, the hell that I was so afraid of was all my fault, so to speak. I heard

many stories and warnings about what kind of woman I should be and what kind of woman I should not be. As a teenage girl growing up inside of Evangelicalism and its regressive sexual ethics, I was taught to fear my own body's desires. I was also taught that anyone else's desire of my body was to be feared—that I was the one to be blamed if someone else desired me.

I deeply internalized the messages I was receiving that my body wasn't safe; those messages were easily the most explicitly stated 'lack of safety' messages relayed to my sense of self up to that point. Within a fundamentalist Christian belief system, people are already raised to believe that the body is sinful and evil, but the messages cisgender women receive about themselves and their sexual identities are even worse. I had heaps and loads of sexual shame and guilt poured onto my developing body and mind. By the time I was a teenager, not only was I terrified of the world around me, but I was also terrified of myself moving in the world.

I then go on in the Creation Story to speak of how these foundational beliefs played a crucial role in the development of my eating disorder:

...Also, in a sense, this [disordered eating] helped me get closer to succeeding at the standard of holiness set for me within my purity culture upbringing. I was afraid to develop, grow, and expand into the 'wrong kind of

woman' by developing hips and breasts that would cause men to sexually desire me. The fear within me of growing larger had two main expressions. Number one, I was afraid of taking up space, occupying the world around me, and having hungers and needs—because of the trauma that my experience with my abusive mother had left me with. Number two, I was afraid of my body developing into the body of a woman, thereby leading men towards sin.

I believed that if I stayed small, I wouldn't anger my mother—or god. My reality of living within an unsafe and abusive home had been so painful, and for years the idea of a god that could love me now that I was saved offered me my only respite. But the fact that I had learned that I could upset that same god by having a specific kind of body, however, filled me with incredible anxiety. I needed god to stay on my team because my felt reality was that no one else was; and the best way to keep god on my team was to remain a pure woman in every way that I could. I had learned for many years that the best way to be a pure woman was to deny yourself the ability to love, take joy, or take pride in your own body because loving that body would only lead to sin.

The beliefs and experience referenced above are rooted in what is known as "purity culture". Purity culture is the name most often used to succinctly describe the Evangelical Christian virginity movement that occurred in the United States from the 1980s through the mid-2000s that attempted to push an agenda of the morality of a "total abstinence until marriage" sexual ethic. Purity culture doesn't just do damage by labeling dating as dangerous, touting marriage as the most important life goal for females, exclusively offering disinformation regarding gender and sex, promoting vast inequality of the sexes, and encouraging abstinence-only education in public schools; the majority of what comes out of the religious rhetoric is wrapped up in language that describes the physical body the root of all that is evil, or "sinful". Natural human desires are described as ungodly and dangerous, and are required to be suppressed until (implied heterosexual) marriage in order to be holy. This was the narrative I was immersed in growing up, but for the majority of my life I did not have any language for the experience I felt happening within me of being systematically coerced into mistrusting—and therefore disassociating from—my own body.

As afraid as I was of the idea of knowing that god, there was within me a much deeper fear of disappointing or angering that god, who had somehow seen fit to murder his own son. Even at such a young age, I was panicked about feeling required to have a strong sense of certainty surrounding beliefs I couldn't even begin to understand or feel safe agreeing to. I learned to fear hell—and my own eternally and inescapably corrupted self—for the very first time. The fear of what was on the other side of failing to do as god said transformed me into a frightened moral perfectionist almost instantly, fueled by a desperate scrupulosity.

Early on, it was imposed upon me that I was only safe to keep company with certain types of other children—specifically Protestant Christian children. I internalized those rules for myself so intensely that I became too afraid to establish any sort of relationship outside of the ones I was trained into believing god allowed. I was taught to be afraid of the influence non-Evangelical people might have upon me, so I became completely terrified of it and of them.

When I was eight or nine years old, I had a major anxiety attack after attending a sleepover at my neighbor's house. I was deeply afraid of the idea of accompanying my neighbors to their Catholic church. I had been told all too often how Catholics were non-Christians and were especially dangerous because they were deceived. I was taught that Catholics thought they knew god, but because they had made an idol of Mary and didn't feel it necessary to pray a specific prayer of salvation "asking Jesus into your heart" they were deceived by satan and going to hell.

That message wasn't enough to make it problematic for me to hang out and play with my neighbors, but when I was invited to spend the night and forgot it was a Saturday I woke up the next day and had an utter meltdown. I was genuinely terrified they were going to take me to their church and I would be brainwashed into becoming a Catholic. I was genuinely terrified that if I attended their church with them, god would think I was one of them and wouldn't let me into heaven when I died. Looking back now, my panic must have been embarrassing for me and extremely insulting to the parents of my friends—sobbing, begging to just be allowed to go home instead.

Eventually, my mom had to come and pick me up to take me home. After she came to get me she told me I was making a big deal out of nothing and it would have been fine for me to go to their church with them. I remember how deeply confusing this was for me as a child, after being told so often that I needed to be fearful of the world outside of our specific Christian bubble and that Satan could deceive me without my knowledge if I spent time in spaces that didn't belong to our god.

Looking back, my panic makes sense—the consequences of being deceived by satan were dire and the stakes were high. In addition to having a sinful nature, I was raised to believe in the eternal conscious punishment that was waiting for everyone who didn't receive our specific kind of salvation. I know now what was never taught to me—that there has always been deep debate occurring amongst individuals and denominations as to whether or not the doctrine of hell is rooted in an incorrect translation of the Christian scripture—but a theological belief in a place of eternal torment after physical death is a core tenet of most Evangelical Christianity. And most frighteningly, it is almost always taught to young children in an effort to convince them to receive salvation in order to return them to right standing with god.

As a teenager, I read a book written by a popular Evangelical pastor about hell but was unable to get through the introduction where he told a story about his grandmother dying without first becoming "saved". He wrote about how even though the knowledge of where she was spending eternity emotionally destroyed him, he was somehow able to arrive at a place of faithful obedience by saying that god's ways and god's sense of justice were far beyond and above his own. In view of his own grandmother being actively tortured for all of eternity, this pastor believed that he simply needed to trust that somehow, her torment spoke to the reality of the goodness of his god.

I remember thinking, even then, that while I knew how he got to that conclusion, I couldn't bring myself to stomach the same. Reading his words took me back to the time when I first learned of hell when I was about seven years old. I was taught I should feel safe and secure because the answers were always that some people were definitely going there because all people definitely deserved it, and yet only a few people would know well enough the proper way to avoid it. What I remember most about this from the entirety of my time within Evangelicalism is that somehow the idea that I alone was escaping hell was sup-

posed to be enough for me to be comfortable with l
ing in it, but due to my naturally empathic nature that explanation was never enough for me.

Because of my deep fear of the very existence of hell—
in addition to the fear of my own sinful nature and of the
impending end of the world—I had vivid nightmares and
anxiety attacks that began when I was very young. I would
cry for my parents to come into my room most nights after
putting me to bed, and I would ask them questions about
heaven and hell, god and the devil, good and evil. I would
express my fear of eternity—a unit of time I couldn't even
begin to conceive of—and they would console me that
because of my blessed assurance in the blood of Jesus, I
was safe from the flames of hell. I'm certain they believed
that my fear was simply rooted in doubt and that rein-
forcing a sense of certainty would offer a cure. But for me,
it was dwelling on the idea that anyone would be going to
hell at all that felt so traumatic. It plagued my conscious
mind constantly.

For many years, the initial feelings from my early conversion experience—the pressure and uncertainty, fear
and coercion—never left. I frequently imagined visions
of people I knew and loved burning in a lake of fire for
an unending length of time. When I was thirteen, I wrote
a poem imagining a not-so-distant future where my best
friend died in a car accident and screamed at me from

her eternal torture that her fate was all my fault because I hadn't done enough to save her. I aptly and painfully titled it, "Reality":

She called me up that evening
And chirped a glad "hello"
She told me about this party
And asked if I wanted to go
I didn't want her to laugh at me
I didn't want to sound dumb
So I compromised and said, "Why not?
Let's go and have some fun!"
I know I should have just said no
And told her of my faith
But that "what would Jesus do" thing's old
For now, Jesus could wait
She came in her car to pick me up
And I climbed into the chair
I told her I liked her outfit
She told me she liked my hair
We saw a truck going crazy
As we went on our way
The driver must have been drunk or something
He was going all over the place
The man swerved off into our lane
And didn't see us, it seems
The last thing I saw was the window crash in
The last thing I heard were her screams
I awoke to the darkness

And called her name out loud
Then I looked over and saw her
Lying lifeless on the ground
There's blood all over my hands now
Tears are stinging my eyes
Of all the thoughts running through my head
I keep thinking of all the "whys"
Why, God, couldn't you take her later?
Why are you taking her at all?
Her future now will never come
The life she lived was so small
Then it hit me—hard
There's even more to this loss
All the while I knew her
I never told her of the cross
I thought she'd never listen
I thought that she'd just laugh
And now as she lay here dead
I knew the time to share had passed
This cannot be happening
I thought I'd have more time
Lord, why did you take her life?
Why couldn't you have taken mine?
I never told her of God's love
Of the death of his only son
And now as I hold her cold, still hand
I knew her life was done
I could just imagine seeing her there

Her soul burning in eternal hell
I could see her reaching out to me
And I could hear her yell
"I always wanted to know," she screamed
"But I was too afraid to ask!
I thought sooner or later you'd tell me.
Didn't your Jesus give you that task?"
Slowly her face began to fade away
As I woke from my dream
Then I realized it wasn't real
But so real did it seem
As I jumped out of bed
Straight to the phone I ran
I called her up and told her
I had to talk to her as soon as I can
I'm telling you right here and now
Don't wait to share Christ with a friend
Because you can never be sure
When their life could come to an end.

This fear over where other human beings could potentially end up for all of eternity was often the fuel for my fire of "sharing the gospel" or evangelism. The practice of evangelism is extremely important to many Evangelical denominations, and my relationship towards it was fairly complicated. We were taught and trained to knock on neighbor's doors, walk up to strangers in shopping malls, and fervently proselytize our own friends and family members in an effort to save their souls. These activities felt uncomfortable and invasive, but also somehow of dire importance, and I was consumed with the reality of the danger that was waiting for all people on the other side of death if I didn't save them.

My natural empathy was paralyzed in the Evangelical paradigm. I thought there must be some deep rooted sin within me causing me to be so resistant to spreading the gospel, and that I needed to repent and be obedient so that I could be used to fulfill god's purpose and mission. As a child and as a teenager, I had an ever-present feeling of shame that followed me for the fact that I hadn't yet converted anyone that I knew. In fact, my biggest regret when my parents removed me from my public school when I was ten years old was that I had wasted my time there by being too ashamed of Jesus to share him with my friends so that they could go to heaven. This debilitating guilt, shame, and fear over the consequences of salvation—or the lack thereof—is where Evangelical belief had always broken down for me, even before I began to break down inside it.

Professor, writer, and well-known former Evangelical Chrissy Stroop talks about their own experience with this sort of damaging theology in their article about spiritual abuse and the conversion of young children. In it, they write:

I know there is a secular world out there. I know some people believe in evolution. But at the moment I'm not thinking about any of that. I'm standing in front of my dresser, my bare feet digging into the shag carpet, staring into the open sock drawer. Perhaps this is not long after the time that my sister and I tried to get our cats to kneel so we could walk them through the sinner's prayer. But why am I standing still, anxious, unable to simply choose a pair of socks and get on with the day? The problem is that I am not sure which pair of socks it is God's will for me to put on. Perhaps if I put on the right pair of socks, it will somehow lead to a conversation in which I can help someone get saved. And what if I fail to listen to the Holy Spirit instead? Will I be punished? Will I be able to live with myself? (Stroop "Break the Cycle")

In order to provide an antidote to humans' inescapable sin nature, the possibility of salvation and/or redemption, and to restore the relationship between humans and the divine, various atonement theories (e.g. ransom theory, christus victor, moral influence, scapegoat theory) emerge. Dominant in Evangelicalism today is penal substitutionary atonement, the notion that Jesus was punished by his father—crucified—on behalf of all human sinners whom god could not abide. This theory centers around a thirst for punishment that the divine has because of his anger towards sin and need for justice.

In this view, it is the death of Jesus—more so than the teachings, life or even resurrection—that is most important. The images and implications of an innocent Jesus suffering and dying to atone for my sinful self to satisfy god's justified wrath at my inescapable wickedness were drilled into me from an early age.

But the way this supposed good news felt within my body was as if Jesus needed to convince this god that I was lovable in the first place. And even then, I was only lovable because of the fact that Jesus did something on my behalf and his blood now "covered" me. Why did someone else's blood have to be spilled to make me lovable, and what did that mean for the ones who either didn't recognize or didn't know to recognize that blood as the only thing that cleaned up their appearance to make them lovable too? Did that make them unlovable? Did that mean we were on opposing teams, and did it make them wrong where I was right? Did that mean that they were wrong and unacceptable in the sight of god in the same way that I was now right and pleasing to him in all things?

In addition, the difficult reality of my own "rightness" was that it was not actually mine. It didn't grow from within me but came from outside of myself, and it was only because of a belief in sin nature in the first place that would make something like this substitution necessary. I could only be pardoned after acknowledging how bad I had been to begin with. The penalty for my sin was written into the songs I repeatedly sang throughout my childhood and even in the poetry I wrote myself. One that I wrote at 14 years old, made my eighth grade English teacher so proud that she submitted it to be included in an anthology of 8th grade student poetry from around the country. It was selected and published, and my parents, teachers, and church leaders told me for weeks how proud they were of me—now that the gospel would be shared with so many people who read the book.

It was because of my lies
The soldiers pushed you to your knees
It was my disobedience
That flogged you with such ease
Because I cheated
They placed a crown of thorns upon your head
I coveted and so
You hung on the cross and were left for dead
Because I cursed
You were spit upon, slapped and wounded, beat
It was my sin and not the nails
That pierced your hands and feet
Because I didn't put God first
People's heads and fists they shook
Because of all the times I've asked, "Why me?"
Death came, your life, it took
Because of all your love for me
You hung on the cross that day
You could have come right off and lived
But instead you decided to stay

Because you accepted me
You breathed your last
It was for that reason that
Your life, it went, it passed
Because you are the son of God
You rose up from the dead
And now instead of a crown of thorns
A crown of gold rests upon your head
Because you are the conquerer
You're coming again someday
And because you loved me enough to die
I praise your holy name

I repeated a belief in this specific redemptive violence over and over myself throughout my childhood, adolescence, and beyond, and unquestioningly internalized the value of wrath to bring about my forgiveness and redemption. When it came to what was responsible for making me whole, my language was solely rooted in fear.

Not only was the god we were taught to believe in violent and jealous, but he was unpredictable and vengeful all while simply biding his time, waiting to destroy the current world and everything in it that didn't worship him in order to create a new world only for those on his team. The warnings in my Evangelical subculture about the "end times" were constant and dire. We had Sunday morning sermons about the approaching end of days and book clubs in which the apocryphal Left Behind series was taken as gospel truth. This inundation resulted in my developing a very specific form of chronic fear called rapture anxiety where I would panic when my parents left the house in case the rapture were to happen, and I wouldn't be taken up to Heaven, but left all alone.

We had a children's choir at the church where I grew up and I remember being taught to sing a specific song called "I Wish We'd All Been Ready" when I was around ten years old. It was a deeply disturbing song to have such a pleasant tune, much less for children to be singing:

Life was filled with guns and war
And all of us got trampled on the floor
I wish we'd all been ready
The children died, the days grew cold
A piece of bread could buy a bag of gold
I wish we'd all been ready
There's no time to change your mind
The son has come and you've been left behind
A man and wife asleep in bed
She hears a noise and turns her head he's gone
I wish we'd all been ready
Two men walking up a hill
One disappears and ones left standing still
I wish we'd all been ready
The father spoke, the demons dined
How could you have been so blind?
There's no time to change your mind
The son has come and you've been left behind
There's no time to change your mind

The son has come and you've been left behind
I hope we'll all be ready
You've been left behind

This song was written about and rooted in the theology of the "rapture"—a belief taken from the book of Revelation in Christian scripture that taught that Jesus was going to return to earth at a certain time in the future, and Christian people would suddenly disappear as they were taken into heaven. The rest of the earth was doomed to consumed in a giant, apocalyptic war that would eventually be won when Jesus conquered Satan and sent him to hell forever—along with all of the people that "served him" (essentially, anyone who wasn't a Christian).

Belief in the rapture caused an enormous amount of anxiety in my brain and body when I was a child. Maybe that's why when my parents went to Hawaii for their tenth anniversary when I was 8 years old, I cried every night they were away fearing they would be taken up into heaven and that I would be left behind. It also probably had something to do with the reason I had an anxiety attack when my father, mother, sister, and brother went out for my dad's birthday one year—leaving myself and my cousin at home with a babysitter—and I kept imagining having to face this giant war all by myself because my entire family would have been taken up into heaven without me.

ears later, during my time in what I would come
to realize was a charismatic Evangelical cult, that violent,
militaristic language became a benchmark in the worship and prayer services that would sometimes go on for
six to eight hours at a time. We were told to believe that
we were being raised up as an army and that we needed
to be "dressed for battle". This church, which was an out-
growth of one of the largest Evangelical ministries in the
United States, preached a doctrine completely enmeshed
in "End Times Theology" and rallied around their belief
that Jesus was returning to earth soon in the form of a
conquering hero with robes that were stained with the
blood of his enemies. It honestly felt as if Jesus was simply perpetuating the violence that had been committed
against himself; upon his return, it would become his job
to kill whomever he deemed were workers of iniquity.

It could be tempting to dismiss those who hold this belief as being nothing more than a fringe group, but my previous community and so many others like them make up
a large sector of Evangelicalism. The language I remember most had threads of religion and politics woven to-
gether as one unified, larger image that was violent, conquering, authoritarian, and imperialistic. We were taught
to believe that individual people who practiced other re-
ligions were a threat because they were actively working
on behalf of the devil. The songs sung and language used
during worship services were about how we were building an army for the one true lord, and how the enemies

of our god were our personal enemies, too—and they deserved to be destroyed. There was active, passionate prayer against other houses of worship, such as temples and mosques, in the neighborhood where we lived. There was zero tolerance for anything other than Christian expressions of worship, and a significant portion of spiritual and emotional energy during services was focused in attempts to direct heavenly forces in their direction for destruction. I didn't even realize until I got out of the cult how obsessively focused my life had become on a belief in "end times " violence ushering in the return of Jesus.

Also to be considered in any conversation about Evangelicalism's relationship towards "redemptive" violence is its strange obsession with corporal punishment, or physical abuse by way of spanking, as a widely accepted disciplinary action towards children. Unfortunately, this was the preferred method of punishment in my Evangelical family and wasn't just used in my home, but in my Christian school as well. It was quite common for disobedient or unruly students in my Christian middle school to be sent to the office to be spanked by the principal. The idea that young children could and should be trained out of disobedient behavior by instilling the fear of physical harm was, and in many spaces still remains, a belief and behavior sanctioned and encouraged by the Evangelical church—in spite of the fact that the American Academy of Pediatrics has now spoken out in full opposition to it (Jenkins & Garcia-Navarro).

Being spanked was my most frequent form of punishment, as my mother made it clear that she thought that any form of discipline that wasn't physically hitting me was going too easy on me. She believed that I had to be spanked in order to keep my sin nature in line, and all of the messages I received from my religion were that this was something god encouraged for both parents and leaders of disobedient children. My parents and teachers would occasionally even pray with me both before and after they hit me, solidifying in my mind that this was god's perfect plan. I eventually learned that this lesson was the one god most often taught, and that pain and suffering was something god used to discipline the children that He loved. This glorification of suffering would later become what I would use within myself to justify my own self-harm.

The times I most clearly remember being hit or physically disciplined were when I hadn't even necessarily misbehaved or "sinned". I was spanked most often for showing negative emotions or a personality trait not deemed desirable—when I would speak up, question authority or assert my boundaries. The simple combination of having a strong personality inside a female body frequently earned me physical pain as retribution. It became clear to me very early on that my lack of a naturally submissive personality presented a very specific problem—and that problem would earn me pain that I somehow innately deserved.

The value of Evangelical corporal punishment comes from a verse in the Old Testament that instructs parents that if they "spare the rod", they hate their children. When taken literally, this verse seems to communicate that faithful parents are justified in committing physical violence against their own children in the name of god. Within such a paradigm, physical abuse is seen as sanctioned, holy, and restorative work, and it bears a deep connection to the belief in original sin. If children are born evil, then their outbursts are not attempts at emotional regulation and their disobedience is not experimental autonomy—it is sin, and the sinful will must be broken. When I was a child, there were hundreds of books extolling the virtue of corporal punishment and spanking. Some of these books went so far as to instruct parents to physically hit their infants if they were emoting too often or too intensely.

Puberty and the beginning of my sexual identity development did not ease the pain and suffering my body experienced but only added more confusion in the midst of purity culture. I was taught for years the most important thing I could do as a woman was be obedient, submissive, mistrust my own body, and dissociate myself from my own sexuality. I would be considered a ruined vessel if I dared engage in any form of sexual activity before marriage. There was no other more significant or important moral evaluation for me as a female apart from whether or not my hymen remained intact for me to give away as the gift of my virginity to a man. I was, along with so many other girls my age, encouraged to make a pledge to god and my father that I would remain pure and not ruin myself before my wedding day.

The problem, however, was that I was already beginning to explore and learn my own body, experiencing sensations that I didn't understand, no one was willing to explain, and I was too afraid to ask about. There was no sex education in my home or my church, and my Christian school only spoke of abstinence. I felt that my genuine curiosity about my body or my genitals would lead me down a path of destruction—ruining me as a woman, as a Christian, and as a potential future wife to a holy man. I was taught that unless I separated myself from my budding sexuality, I would never be happy or used by god. My internalized shame over my own body's development and natural curiosity made me believe that I had to be at war with myself in order to become a good woman who was no longer curious about herself, her body, sensations, pleasures, or desires.

Over time, I became convinced that my inability to drive my own sexuality out of me must mean that my sexuality was uncontrollable and that I needed to seek professional help. The fact that I felt an undeniable biological impulse towards engaging with my sexuality at all must make me an addict—or so I believed. So while it was the one area of my life where I felt like my truest self when I was engaging with it and expressing it, every moment of engagement or expression itself was deeply traumatizing because I believed I was committing the worst possible sin. Every day felt like I had split myself into two different women, and was ripping myself apart because the only way I could succeed was to somehow manage for my required identity to function completely apart from the honest one.

I quite literally thought and felt that I would never be good, correct, moral, or holy simply because of the existence of my sexuality. Purity culture had long convinced me that there was no greater measure of my character or worth than if I remained utterly unsexual and virginal until my wedding day. I felt like I would lose everything my life was supposed to be about unless I somehow managed to separate myself completely from my sexual identity and impulses and the stress of this inner battle consumed me. It affected the way I interacted with and treated my body at every turn, and I became captive to disordered eating patterns and habitual self-harm because I was terrified of having a body that I took pleasure in, enjoyed, and was proud of—because if I did, I was to bound use that body for sin. I prayed often to be emptied out of all of my desires—the foremost of which was begging for my sexual desires to be removed. Out of devotion, I developed a taste for restriction since desiring, craving, and wanting was sinful.

What's fascinating to me now is that as much anxiety as my religious beliefs clearly caused me, they were intangible and imaginary at time in my life when my tangible reality was too much to bear. So the belief itself became an escape. As a child, my days felt frightening—I was unsafe in my home because of my mother's anger and I was bullied in school and had precious few interactions with friends that didn't result in being mocked or made fun of. Consequently, I spent a lot of my time alone and tried to be outside of my house as much as possible.

Being afraid of god was one thing; imagining that the god who was so frightening was on my team instead of against me was another—I made that god my only team member, and I dedicated myself to pleasing him so I wouldn't lose him too. No matter how cruel, confusing, or abusive that god was to me or to others, it didn't matter. I couldn't lose that god. So I let that god do all sorts of things to me in my own head, and let that god tell other people to do all sorts of things to me. I let that god tell my parents to hit me because they loved me. I let that god tell me that my mind couldn't be trusted and was corrupted by evil spirits—so I was terrified of engaging with entertainment, experiences, and relationships that weren't overtly Evangelical. I let that god be the recipient of letters in the form of journal entries where I told that god that I wanted to empty myself of all of my desires for my own life; that I would try my hardest to become less selfish for wanting friends, a boyfriend, or a safe home with loving parents because suffering is a sign of discipline and that god disciplines the ones he loves. So he must really love me.

I let god be the reason why I said no to things that brought me pleasure, because if I were to love any part of my life or even my own body more than I loved that god, that god would punish me or worse—leave me. Because whoever loves their own life loses it, and self-esteem is evil; you must have god-esteem. I let that god be the promised reward for my hatred of my own physical body. After all, the less I clung to myself and my own needs, the more he would be glorified. He must increase, I must decrease; and decrease I did.

It was the chronically internalized fear and shame involved in being in relationship with that god that caused my own traumatic experience by steadily eroding my sense of safety. Because this was happening consistently, repeatedly, and systemically, two expectations of the human experience manifested within me: 1. That this was the way it will always be, and 2. That this was the way it was supposed to be. The spiritual and religious abuse of my fundamentalist Evangelical belief upheld certainty as the highest law. In a strange sense, it was less important what I was certain of—just that I was completely certain. That same pivot I made to "this is the way it is supposed to be" is something former Evangelicals often admit they did to themselves by believing that if they both claimed and projected a sense of certainty, the certainty would eventually appear. But in my experience, in order to arrive at that place of certainty, my emotions, reactions, and self-advocacy had to be disposed of.

When I left the cult I had found my way into in my mid-twenties, the specific abuse inflicted upon me by that community was rooted in their belief that anything less than a positive response to pain was disobedient and unfaithful to god and his design. When they uprooted me, left me with no home or form of income, and relationally abandoned me for the sake of continuing to focus on building their project with the people that were there, it was both implied and directly stated that it was now my job to be obedient and faithful to both them and god because this is what god knew and intended to have happen all along—they were simply the arbiters of his perfect will.

I felt lonely, afraid, depressed—I plummeted deeper into cycles of self-harm that had offered themselves to me as pain-avoiding compulsions, but I couldn't say a word. Not only to them, but to anyone else. I had staked my entire life upon this specific shot at a sense of certainty. To express grief, upset, disappointment, or worst of all anger over what had been done to me would have been to give myself away as an unfaithful, double-minded individual, unfit for service in building the kingdom of god.

Ironically and unluckily, I knew that movement well. Returning to a state of unexpressed fear over my own wellbeing and shame over the fact that that fear existed in the first place was like heading home to an abusive lover. It was alarmingly easy to do at 26 years old when I had been writing poems at 16 years old about how god disciplines those he loves, so the more pain I felt, the more I knew god had big plans for me—the one he must have so wildly loved. But as it is said: "when you sweep an emotion under the rug, you sweep it into the nervous system". Bottled emotions are not neutral—they go somewhere. There are consequences to believing that this is the way it will always be and this is the way it is supposed to be when this way is rooted in chronic shame and a constant lack of safety.

For myself and so many others, the abuse of this belief begins in the body. It begins in those messages believers are taught about their sin nature, their thought life, their lustful flesh, their uncontrollable dark desires. This begins inside of the physical body when individuals are told that their flesh is at war with their spirit and the flesh needs to be conquered and killed. This particularly takes hold in adolescence when those teachings about abstinence and purity take center stage. Normal, budding desires for intimacy, connection, pleasure, and sensuality, are painted as dark, evil, and dirty—the worst of all sins.

To engage with your sexuality outside of Christian heterosexual marriage is to place your entire future in jeopardy. For years after my first experience using an object to masturbate with at age twelve, I panicked that I would never find a man that would want to be my husband because I had broken my own hymen and ruined myself by "ruining" the virginity that was supposed to be a gift to him. I imagined conversations with my hypothetical potential future husband where I would apologize for taking what was rightfully his, but in my imaginings he would always ultimately reject me because of what I had done.

While this may sound ridiculous or possibly not even that big of a deal, it's important to recall that for a girl growing up in Evangelicalism, the only option available to me for stability was submission as a wife to an Evangelical man. Pursuing an education or becoming a working woman were largely discouraged—and are discouraged even still today. This idea may sound old fashioned, but for so many cisgender girls and women it is very much alive and well within that belief paradigm. So, if one of those women were to compromise her "purity", she would effectively be compromising her entire future. While that may not be true according to what we know of actual opportunities for women in 2019 in the Western world, that doesn't mean it isn't true to her and to her experience of what she had been taught and indoctrinated to believe inside the Evangelical subculture. These girls and women hold a very specific fear in their bodies, the same way I did. We hold it, internalize it, and then eventually even make that felt sense of shame a goal to aspire to—using it as a true north for the cycle of sin and repentance that is held up as so vital to purity and holiness.

Over time, I developed a strange and unhealthy comfort with feelings of shame in my physical body. It didn't take long for this to deepen into a comfort with feelings of actual disgust and hatred for my physical body. The more I hated my body and all of Her sensations and emotions, and the more uncomfortable or even disgusted my own body made me feel, the closer I was to ridding myself of my curse of sin; and the closer I was to the safety of being chosen by a man looking for a godly and pure wife. Hating myself was the ticket in; punishing my own body for what She wanted was the only way to make Her stop wanting. There is only one definition strong enough and accurate enough for this experience: religious trauma.

RELIGIOUS
TRAUMA + PTSD

The numbers are clear—a significant number of people are rapidly leaving Evangelical Christianity. According to the Pew Religious Landscape Study, over 25% of US adults identified as Evangelicals in 2014. While total religious affiliation dropped dramatically between 2007 and 2014 (nearly 8%), Evangelical Christianity had a slower decline of only about 1% ("America's Changing Religious Landscape"). By 2017, however, the Public Religion Research Institute (PRRI) was reporting a greater decrease of 6% between 2006 and 2016 of people who identify as white Evangelical Christians stating, "Fewer than one in five (17%) Americans are white Evangelical Protestant, but they accounted for nearly one-quarter (23%) in 2006. Over the same period, white Catholics dropped five percentage points from 16% to 11%, as have white mainline Protestants, from 18% to 13%" (Cox & Jones, "America's Changing Religious Identity").

The former paradigm of American religious devotion is dying. I believe this exodus is not just due to the changing political, cultural, and social landscape of our modern world. Nor is it solely because of what the presidential election of Donald Trump revealed to many who were either unable or unwilling to see it before. I believe the primary explanation for this shift is because our societal understanding of trauma, its manifestations and its effects, is growing. People are becoming more equipped to identify their personal psychological and physiological experiences within the definition of trauma itself. As our culture becomes significantly more trauma-informed in language and understanding, people are more able to recognize their symptoms and identify their triggers. As individuals are increasingly able to pay more attention to their body and mind and have greater freedom of access to the information that scientific research offers, they are waking up to their intuitive wisdom telling them to seek safety and leave authoritarian, abusive, and traumatic institutions.

Terms like Religious Trauma Syndrome have entered into public conversation. Almost every day, I encounter folks in "Exvangelical" spaces both in person and on-line who, upon learning the term for the first time, feel incredible relief in their body, mind, and spirit to learn that their singular experiences have a name—and can be deservingly classified as trauma. Once they know how to define what happened to them, most often they can't go back. I believe that massive numbers of people are leaving Evangelicalism because they are being given the permission to understand the manifestations of their trauma—whether or not they even consciously knew it upon their departure.

This psychological and physiological experience is known as Religious Trauma Syndrome, or RTS, and is a relatively new clinical diagnosis coined by psychologist Dr. Marlene Winell. This is the term most survivors of Evangelicalism are looking for but very often don't know they need—or that it even exists. RTS is the condition experienced by people who are struggling with leaving an authoritarian, dogmatic religion and coping with the damage of indoctrination (Winell, Religious Trauma Syndrome). While the term does not exclusively apply to Evangelical Christians, that was Dr. Winell's personal experience being raised by fundamentalist Christian missionary parents. RTS is a function of both the chronic abuses of harmful religion and the impact of severing one's connection with one's faith, and it can be easily compared to a combination of PTSD and Complex PTSD (C-PTSD).

Awareness of how the brain processes events and experiences, and how the body responds, has increased immensely and resulted in a greater social sensitivity to adverse experiences. Researchers have come to recognize that trauma is an impactful psychophysical experience—even if the original event/on-going experience does not necessarily threaten to cause any direct bodily harm (Rothschild 5). In other words, the conversation about trauma has become more subjective. After all, who can define what is disturbing about an experience better than the individual having the specific experience themselves? What one person finds distressing, another may not, and an awareness of that subjectivity is crucial to any attempt to understand the full reality of religious trauma.

Peter Levine very simply states in *Waking the Tiger* that trauma need not be obviously traumatic to be traumatizing. Trauma is determined by how the body responds to an incident, not the actual incident itself (Levine 128). The psychological response to an on-going experience may have greater psycho/physiological consequence than the nature of the event itself, and it is that subsequent response that initiates the potential for the development of PTSD. Trauma occurs when any event or situation creates an unresolved impact on an organism and can be quite succinctly defined as an "overwhelming event". It is an individual person's unique threshold for what is "overwhelming" that determines the development of Post Traumatic Stress and eventually PTSD.

The causes of RTS, as outlined by Winell, come by way of a combination of toxic theology and authoritarianism received and reinforced at church, school, and in the home. These causes include the suppression of normal child development wherein the cognitive, social, emotional, and moral stages are affected, as well as damage to normal thinking and feeling abilities because of the way independent thinking and feelings are condemned and the way information is limited and controlled (Winell, "Religious Trauma Syndrome"). Additionally, as Winell points out, under Evangelicalism, control is external to the individual person, knowledge is revealed (not discovered) and enforced by a hierarchy of authority while the individual self is not believed to be reliable or safe. Finally, both the repression of sexuality and the administration of corporal punishment during formative years can be identified as physical and sexual abuse ("Religious Trauma Syndrome").

Dr. Winell also points out that it is so difficult to break free from this form of belief because it is cyclical in nature. She states that the "doctrines of original sin and eternal damnation cause the most psychological distress by creating the ultimate double bind" wherein the individual is found to be innately guilty by no fault of their own, but is not capable or allowed to do anything about it ("Religious Trauma Syndrome"). This creates a reliance upon a commitment to a conflicted mental state until death, and keeps the believer in an unending cycle of shame and relief. Unfortunately, even in attempting to stop the cycle by leaving the belief system, many do not find the relief they desperately need because the vast psychological damage does not go away overnight. The fear of hell, especially, can sometimes last an entire lifetime, despite cognitive dismissal, and the long-term damage to self-esteem and self-trust can affect a survivor for years after departure ("Religious Trauma Syndrome").

RTS can be extremely difficult to recognize, often because it is frequently mistaken for other disorders such as anxiety, depression, bipolar, OCD, BPD, eating disorders, sexual dysfunction, substance abuse, or various antisocial behaviors. The symptoms of RTS have long been mistakenly viewed as entirely unrelated to religious doctrine. The symptoms found in cognitive, emotional, social, and cultural expressions can include poor critical thinking ability, low self-worth and self-esteem, perfectionism, extreme dualistic thinking, difficulty with pleasure, loss of meaning, loneliness, depression, anxiety, and unnamed grief ("Religious Trauma Syndrome"). Additionally, many people experience social awkwardness, sexual difficulty, loss of social network or family unit, unfamiliarity with the "secular" world, difficulty relating to others or feeling a sense of belonging, and strange gaps in information due to their previously restricted access to information ("Religious Trauma Syndrome").

Religious Trauma is also difficult to recognize or validate in the mental health world because of the cultural assumptions that religion does more good than harm and that belief is universally beneficial. Not all forms of belief deserve to be viewed in this way—Evangelicalism is dangerous because its teachings require belief in and acceptance of things that are psychologically and behaviorally maladaptive and easily lead to extremism. It erodes the natural contentment and confidence, the healthy human needs with which most children begin life and is particularly problematic for developing minds (Winell 5). The authoritarian aspect of Evangelicalism is what is especially problematic, as it communicates that all that is good, sacred, or correct is external to you and everything internal is considered bad. This position fosters deep codependence and mistrust of self and offers no permission or access to inner resources (Winell 5).

Additionally, the spiritual deconstruction phase of the experience of RTS can often be very a confusing time— encompassing a mix of heavy and light, exhilaration and fear, loneliness and freedom. For many, losing god feels like losing a parent, and that loss has the potential to be devastating (Winell 4). The loss of god is an extremely complicated grief. People feel shame for their grief, believing they should be able to get over the loss of god quickly or they should not feel so devastated. They may feel that their devotion was simply a set of cognitive beliefs, when in reality their belief had deep emotional and relational impact.

Unlike many authentic spiritual expressions and the environments of many moderate religious groups, Evangelicalism offers a precarious foundation upon which individuals attempt to build their sense of self. Many spaces of more moderate faith and spirituality respect individual differences, support people in the development of their own self-esteem, remain open to outside influence and connection, and are tolerant of and curious about other faiths (Winell 6). Evangelicalism requires followers to reject the potential value of other faith systems and takes their own scripture as the only true, literal, inspired word of the Divine—resulting in an extreme exclusivity. It is also exudes the language of judgement as it relates to the existence of heaven and hell which results in many people living and moving through the world with a deep sense of fear and anxiety held inside their bodies.

For those raised to believe its doctrines are ultimate truths, and for the society impacted by its political clout, the consequences are serious (Winell 6). Here in the United States, dualistic thinking dominates political institutions, there is a deep cultural assumption that personal value must be competed for, and the use of violence as a redemptive force runs deep (Winell 6). Historically and culturally this society has encouraged individuals to seek validation of their worth outside of themselves, and fostered and exploitative relationship with the earth and natural resources (Winell 6). All of these cultural values are deeply rooted in the patriarchal, authoritarian construct that is fundamentalist, Evangelical Christianity.

The exclusivity and authoritarianism of belief systems like Evangelicalism result in disconnection—from self, from other people, and from the outside world. Those within and those in recovery after leaving are deeply scarred by their experiences. By focusing completely on the virtues of god, of another world, and of the future, fundamentalism and other similar systems create separation and distance from what we need to know and experience as humans (Winell 8). What has become more and more apparent to me is that the core doctrines and teachings of fundamentalist Evangelicalism are extremely traumatic because they distort the way the human psyche would naturally function and thrive. I cannot help but wonder if the only individuals who appear not to be traumatized are the ones still able to convince themselves of the accuracy of those core teachings—possibly because they are compensating for their trauma in unhealthy ways, most often through compulsive behavior and addictive patterns.

The complicated issue with this assertion is that the doctrines of depravity and original sin keep traumatized individuals locked into a closed loop; compulsive, self-destructive patterns are seen as confirmation of a "sin nature" from birth rather than the symptoms of the psycho/physical trauma believers accrue daily. It's an extremely dangerous cycle, but an extremely effective one in creating passive, dependent, and emotionally unbalanced human beings who are more easily manipulated and controlled. This is why, for many who have left this religious narrative, the process of leaving began with "doubt" in one area of doctrine (belief in hell, sin nature, etc.) and this is also why the narrative in the belief system surrounding doubt vs. faith is so tightly controlled.

The more I study and work with recovering individuals and the further away from the belief system I personally get, the less willing I become to give this belief system any form of validation. I refuse to speak softly on this. Fundamentalist Evangelicalism is toxic, traumatic, and extremely dangerous. Those of us who have found our way out are not rare cases where healthy doctrine was simply expressed in an unhealthy manner (i.e., "imperfect people serving a perfect god", etc.), though our individual experiences may vary in levels of intensity. We are indicative of the greater, underlying dysfunction of the entire system.

To understand why RTS is a form of PTSD, we need to understand the mechanisms of PTSD itself. When facing a threat, the brain signals the Autonomic Nervous System (ANS), comprised of the Sympathetic Nervous System (SNS) that primes us for fight or flight, and the Parasympathetic Nervous System (PNS) that helps lower heart and breathing rates. If trauma is prolonged and the body can't or simply doesn't choose to fight or flee, this often results in a third and maladaptive response: freeze—wherein the limbic system activates both the SNS and PNS, immobilizing the body (Rothschild 9).

PTSD is a complex psychobiological condition and often emerges in the wake of perceived life threatening experiences when the psychological and physiological stress responses persist long after the traumatic event has ended (Rothschild 6). People with PTSD typically have lower cortisol levels in their bodies, indicating that their adrenal glands were not able to release enough cortisol to halt the alarm reaction occurring in the ANS when they were experiencing threat (Rothschild 9). PTSD disrupts normal functioning for those suffering from it and often interferes with their ability to perform basic tasks to meet their daily needs (Rothschild 9).

Most often, PTSD develops in an individual in response to 3 types of events:

1. Incidents that are or are perceived as threatening to one's own life or bodily integrity.

2. Witnessing acts of violence to others.

3. Sometimes simply hearing of violence to or the unexpected or violent death of close associates (Rothschild 7).

The symptoms associated with PTSD include avoiding reminders of the incident of trauma including speaking about it, re-experiencing the event in varying sensory forms in the here and now, and a state of chronic hyperarousal within the autonomic nervous system (Rothschild 7).

It is becoming increasingly clear that the predominant determining factor in predicting the eventual development of PTSD is whether or not dissociation occurred during a traumatic event, as dissociation directly correlates with the deployment of the freeze response in the face of threat (Rothschild 13). When the body freezes rather than fights or flees, it is not able to release the internal energy that builds up within it during the moment the internal alarm system sounds and the ANS is activated. It is normal and healthy for the limbic system to activate the ANS the moment a threat is perceived, with the expectation of energetic expulsion. When the ANS continues to be aroused once a threat is passed however, the energy remains trapped and stagnant within the body (Rothschild 12). When that occurs, it feels to the individual that the traumatic event exists outside of time and is perceived as being still present, rather than in the past. Because of this, the trauma is prevented from occupying its proper position in the past and doesn't feel "over." That sensory experience is at the heart of the condition of PTSD.

When someone is experiencing PTSD, their ability to orient towards safety and away from danger—even in attempting to differentiate between internal cues—decreases (Rothschild 14). Many people, objects, feelings, and sensations are perceived as dangerous, and sometimes possibly even the entire environment itself. I have seen this reality play out with clients who had lost the ability to tell the difference between the negative feeling of anxiety and the positive feeling of excitement as either occurs within their bodies. When daily, sensational reminders of potential threat become prolonged or extreme, the dissociation can become so debilitating that those with PTSD can become severely socially restricted, afraid to leave their own homes, or distrusting of their own physical bodies (Rothschild 14).

Transversely for many, however, PTSD can m... as a feeling of numbness within their bodies, inability to access their emotions, and an emptiness or deadness in their lives (Rothschild 15). Because of the vast differences in the potential manifestations of PTSD, it can be difficult to recognize and can be misdiagnosed as a personality disorder or mental health issue unrelated to trauma. Arguably a good reason for how often this occurs is related to the innate subjective nature of trauma—many people who have experienced things that their brains and bodies processed as traumatic don't actually know that they're allowed to qualify what happened to them as "trauma."

Ultimately, the two factors that determine trauma are the response to an event and whether or not the body was able to seek an energetic resolution by way of that response—not the nature of the event itself. Furthermore, what we know to be true as the study of this field progresses forward, is that any potentially traumatizing event—whether real or imagined—may result in the same physiological responses indicative of PTSD. In other words, you don't necessarily need to physically experience a place of eternal conscious punishment to be traumatized; being told it exists and imagining what it could be like may suffice. One of the most important insights regarding trauma to have come out of the Adverse Childhood Experiences Study was the discovery that when an individual has spent formative, developmental years in an environment that is causing them to live in a state of fear, they tend to dissociate—or freeze in the face of their threat—in order to survive the experience. When an individual feels fear but has no permission or opportunity to express it, discharge it, or seek safety from it, they are almost certain to develop and experience C-PTSD.

Rothschild writes that "upsetting emotions, disturbing body sensations, and confusing behavior impulses can all exist in implicit memory without any conscious access to the information surrounding the context in which they arose or what they are about" (31). For this reason, a reclamation of an individual's connection to their own body, as well as their intuition, is crucial to healing trauma, as I discuss in the final section. What we do know for certain is this: at the root of the development of PTSD is unresolved trauma in the mind and body that was initiated by the freeze response in the face of perceived threat. The energy that would have been expelled by either the fight or flight response remains in the body, and the individual who suffers from PTSD requires, as Peter Levine says, "the healing of trauma through the discharge of energy" (Levine 99)

As for how this relates to Religious Trauma Syndrome: if what determines the development of PTSD is an individual perceiving and experiencing an inability to escape a threatening situation, the insular nature of Evangelical subculture must be considered. Not only is the suppression of most emotions encouraged and enforced, but true escape from teaching that feels threatening isn't possible for many people—particularly children and adolescents. There is truly nowhere to run or hide from what you are told is an eternal reality, an unchangeable inner nature, or an all seeing god. The kind of religious trauma I experienced is repeated and inescapable and causes cycles of paralysis followed by dysfunctional compensatory behaviors.

There is an increasingly large body of current research focused on disseminating how trauma expresses itself in the physical body and the physiological consequences and implications for traumatic or overwhelming experiences. When it comes to complex trauma and the development of PTSD, typically people who suffer from PTSD are missing explicit information that they need in order to make sense of distressing or confusing body sensations and somatic symptoms—many of which are implicit memories of their past trauma (Rothschild 44). One of the primary goals of trauma therapy is for individuals to understand their bodily sensations, and remember how to interpret them. They must first feel and identify the somatic sensations, and develop language to name and describe them in order to heal.

The difficulty in this, however, is that the part of the brain that is responsible for helping the body complete the trauma cycle by providing context to the experience is the same part of the brain that develops verbal language—the hippocampus. It is also the part of brain where activity is suppressed during a traumatic or overwhelming experience, and stays suppressed in cases of PTSD. Developing language is crucial to healing, not only to be able to speak about what happened but also to be able to verbally express sensations and emotional experiences in the body. Often times, the marker of a traumatized person is that when asked how they feel or how an emotion feels within their body, they tell you what they think or what they cognitively know about that emotion instead.

People with PTSD live in a chronic state of hyperarousal, or ANS activation, not just in their brains, but in their bodies as well. This state of hyperarousal leads to symptoms such as anxiety, panic, weakness, exhaustion, muscle stiffness, concentration problems, and sleep disturbances (Rothschild 47). Adaptive techniques that were first developed for survival can over time become the root of impairment. This is because, in cases of PTSD, neutral stimulus becomes dissociated from the present and attached to the incomplete, traumatic memory of the past, resulting in that chronic state of hyperarousal. People with PTSD live with a strange, simultaneous awareness and confusion when it comes to the state of their bodies—aware that their bodies are acting in certain extreme ways, but completely unaware as to the reason why.

Practically, the symptoms of PTSD that can be developed and expressed in the body include both mental and behavioral disturbances, as well as a vast range of physical imbalances. Many people experience insomnia, nightmares, anxiety, depression, memory issues, and an overall feeling of numbness that negatively affect their daily functioning. In addition, they can begin to notice an increase in irritability, poor communication skills, a desire for social isolation, hypervigilance, and various compulsive tendencies to serve as coping mechanisms. Physical manifestations of trauma include extreme weight fluctuation, migraines, difficulty breathing, chronic muscle or joint pain, vomiting, chronic fatigue, digestive issues, poor circulation, and skin rashes. It is also very common to see chronic illness and suppressed immunological function in people suffering from PTSD as well as various forms of sexual dysfunction. Many people with PTSD complain of a low sex drive because sexual arousal "mimics the physiological experience of fear" (Dolan "Post-traumatic stress").

These physical manifestations of trauma can be especially confusing for the individuals experiencing them because they have learned to dissociate from their bodily sensations and somatic information, leaving them disconnected from their own bodies and unfamiliar with their own internal information. They find themselves unable to connect with the deep, inner wisdom necessary for the development of resilience and their own autonomous identity. Re-association to the physical body and to the intuitive self requires an understanding of and a restored ability to communicate with the body and interpret somatic signals. Body signals cue the awareness of the emotional world, and the evolutionary function of emotions that are associated with survival (Rothschild 59).

It has been observed that women and children are more prone to engage the freeze response in the face of threat than to fight or flee, implying that people who feel physically, situationally, or relationally vulnerable are more likely to enact the freeze response and feel immobilized or helpless in the face of their fear. How an individual instinctively responds to life-threatening situations depends on many factors, including their physical and psychological resources (Rothschild 50). In some cases, it takes only one traumatic incident where defensive behavior was either impossible or unsuccessful for it to be wiped from an individual's protective repertoire (Rothschild 54). In other words: being exposed to something that causes deep fear only one time, but combined with inability to escape, will almost inevitably be stored in body as trauma. This means that the individuals in our society who have the least cultural permission to express anger, the least ability to physically defend themselves, and the least practical ability to care for themselves on their own run the highest risk of developing PTSD in the face of adverse experiences.

My experience growing up extremely Evangelical and my commitment to the ideology over two decades of my life both determined and reinforced aspects of my development. To add to my sense of threat and danger, I was raised by an abusive mother. For a long time, in my pursuit of healing, I thought my trauma was solely rooted in my relationship with my mother. As I walked down my years-long path to heal it, however, I began to recognize the overlap of symptoms from my parental abuse and my religious abuse. Fascinatingly, when my body began speaking to me about healing in one area, the other started to unravel and reveal itself as traumatic, too. My home life growing up and my entire experience in Evangelical spaces mirrored one another in the sense that I never achieved a felt sense of safety within my body in either space the entire time I was there, but that acknowledgement wouldn't come until after many years of healing and recovery.

Repetitive beliefs instilled during formative years imprint upon the individual and are the ones through which the individual continues to develop. While it would be interesting to consider the effect of these specific beliefs upon people who came to the Evangelical faith later in life—especially vulnerable individuals who were attracted to the religion because of its false promise to alleviate suffering—I believe the primary question of potential impact lies in the minds and bodies of adult survivors of this form of abusive teaching they received as children and teenagers.

Religious abuse has shaped survivors' brains, language, embodied experiences and sensations, and emotional recognition and regulation. Threatening doctrines attached either guilt or freedom, stress or calm, to specific embodied sensations—and, in some cases, even thought processes. Their abuse imprinted upon them the same way both my religious and parental abuse imprinted upon me. And in order to heal from both, I had to release myself from the environment, establish a felt sense of safety, and give myself permission to believe a different story about myself, the world, and god.

I believe that people need to know that what they were taught to believe under Evangelical doctrine can legitimately be defined as trauma. I believe that the doctrine passed on by parents, teachers, pastors, and educators who may have meant their best ultimately did deep harm. Ill-intention is not a prerequisite for trauma or pain. Similarly, my mother herself was a victim of abuse, and I may never know if her intentions towards me were genuinely cruel or if she simply did the best she was able to do. Regardless, what I experienced with her was abusive and my experience of her throughout my childhood and adolescence is valid. In the same way, the ones who love us may have done their best but still caused harm with their Evangelical beliefs.

There are ways to help survivors recognize that the physical and psychological reactions resulting from trauma are messages—attempts from the body to try and explain what has happened. Imbalances, illnesses, anxieties, and pains are signal flares from our deeper selves searching for rescue. Bessel van der Kolk writes that emotional abuse and neglect can be just as devastating as physical abuse and sexual molestation (van der Kolk 90). He also states that in order to heal, we must have an understanding of the source of the wound (van der Kolk 91). In studying and researching the realities of neurological development, it became apparent to me that there are distinct disadvantages for individuals who were born into and raised among fundamentalist Evangelical belief narratives.

As noted above, in early childhood—when so much about brain chemistry and behavior is being determined by internal responses to external experiences—being raised with frightening and apparently inescapable beliefs can result in the kind of trauma that is often neither recognized nor recovered from easily. Children encouraged—or required—to believe their body is evil instead of good and that they cannot trust themselves have had imprinted upon them a particular way of viewing themselves and the world around them because of the ways their brains developed through their early years of receiving these messages. This is an understanding I arrived at by seeing the similarities between the abuse I experienced with my mother during my formative years, and the patterns I see emerge in people who spent childhood and adolescent years as Evangelicals.

The trauma I developed because of the abuse I received from my mother made me unable to neurologically develop a healthy attachment style. Because of this, throughout the majority of my adult life, I experienced every argument, every break-up, every relocation of a friend, every time someone didn't call when they said they would as life-altering abandonment, rejection, and loss. I was being re-traumatized in every one of those moments and relationships because of the way my early experiences with my mother had imprinted upon me and—unbeknownst to me—predetermined the way that I would be able to establish relationship and connection with others.

So often, for those raised within Evangelical environments, any single moment of perceived failure, any mistake, any step outside the previously established lines can paralyze with life-altering fear, anxiety, shame, and dread because the trauma of early teaching is essentially playing on a loop within us. Our brains developed in a state of restriction, hesitation, and lack rather than a state of permission, wholeness, and freedom. This is why any misstep threatens identity, threatens worthiness, and threatens belonging—because of being raised on such thin ice in relation to our human nature and the whims of an abusive deity that Jesus had to come and pacify to prevent from harming, torturing, and abusing us forever. When raised to believe that, left to our own devices, we deserve to be punished and tortured forever, worthiness, belonging, and safety are entirely conditional; our comfort with our own identity is conditional. Pleasure becomes dangerous, pain becomes discipline, and discipline masquerades as love.

In Trauma and Recovery, the recovery process from traumatic experiences is given in three steps: to establish safety, to reconstruct the story relating to trauma, and to restore the traumatized individual's connection to themselves and others (Herman 3). For my own part, in order to heal from my experience with my mother, I had to release myself from the abusive environment, feel the safety and permission to believe a different story about myself, and reconnect with myself and others I was in relationship with through that new story. Eventually, I came to realize that same method was the identical recovery process I had gone through with my former religious belief as well.

Evangelicalism promises safety and security yet its teachings drive believers into states of fear and helplessness. The foundational doctrine of penal substitutionary atonement celebrates helplessness because it insists the divine enter and act on behalf of helpless humanity. God saves believers by way of redemptive violence because they cannot save themselves. And if the believers are emotionally affected by imagining what eternal damnation might actually entail, they are rebuked, or their fears dismissed. I not only experienced this as "My Story", but also had parents, leaders, and teachers tell me that my emotional responses indicated that I was either disobedient or taking things too seriously. Aside from physical punishment, to have all natural human reactions to frightening doctrines rejected as sin or lack of faith, is akin to undergoing emotional torture.

The contradictions of this kind of emotional suppression are exacerbated when the child is not allowed to question foundational fundamentalist "doctrines". In my case, I was not able to respond to the trauma of my own belief system with "fight". Similarly, I was not able to leave my family, my social structure, and the cultural narrative of how the world and everything in it is organized and therefore I couldn't respond to the constant threat of the belief system with "flight". The only option available to me was "freeze": to stay, to keep staying, and in order to keep staying—to keep suppressing my internal turmoil and experience of trauma.

When I speak to those people who are hard on themselves for staying so long inside a system that they now see clearly was actively harming them, I try to help them recognize that their distinct tonic immobility makes sense in light of how very little agency they had. When constantly traumatized by abusive doctrines, and unable to resist or leave, the entire organism is in a prolonged and largely unvoiced state of stress—leading to mental and emotional imbalance wrapped up in fear, panic, shame, and guilt.

Bodily Impact

In Dr. Paul Martin's work, *The Healing Mind*, he tells of a series of Iraqi missile attacks against Israel during the Gulf War wherein a great number of Israeli citizens died. The curious thing about these deaths, however, was that the vast majority of them did not occur because of any direct physical impact of the missiles themselves (Martin 3). The majority of the people died on the first day of the attack—from heart failure due to the stress, anxiety, and fear brought on by the impending doom of the assault. It was the world that was created by fear—a world they were suddenly required to live in against their power or will—that brought harm to their minds and ultimately their bodies as well. What brought the most harm was not the physical damage caused by the missile attack, but the emotional response that the potentiality of the attack prompted in them.

So what, exactly, does this story have to do with the harm of Evangelicalism? Nearly everything. No one was killed by the missiles themselves on the first day of the attack, and yet that day had the highest death toll. As Martin writes, "The evidence consistently pointed to one conclusion: the sharp rise in death rate... was primarily a consequence of severe emotional stress brought on by fear... It was the psychological impact of the SCUD missiles, and not their physical impact that claimed the majority of the victims" (Martin 3). Not only does psychological trauma, by way of a perceived threat, set the stage for the development of dissociation and PTSD, but it is clear from this story that there are potentially disastrous physiological consequences as well.

When talking about "abuse", Evangelicals in power are often quick to dismiss the effects on those claiming spiritual and religious abuse by focusing exclusively on the "scientifically known" effects of extreme cases of sexual or physical abuse. I am in no way attempting to dismiss or invalidate those who have had those extreme experiences. I am attempting to present a wider vision by asserting that those who focus too much on extreme examples never leave space for the conversation to shift rightly back to the original focus of what we mean when we say "spiritual abuse" or "religious trauma"—that the poison is in the message itself.

The daily world and anticipated eternal horror created by the doctrines of Evangelical Christianity can inflict harm upon those trapped in that world because they live in a constant state of dread or panic from which they can have no escape except into eternal damnation. And perhaps because Christian viewpoints so permeate conversations in the US, most people do not think to question whether extremist Christian beliefs may be as damaging as any other extremist doctrine. Hence people do not recognize that the Evangelical power structure is churning out walking wounded at an alarming rate.

The refugees of these doctrines often cannot seem to connect to themselves, their bodies, or to other people. Many of them experience anxiety, depression, and panic that they aren't able to explain, and they don't feel the inner permission to own their emotions, trust themselves, find peace, or experience pleasure. And many of these same refugees are living and moving in this world carrying unexplained sickness, disease, and imbalance for which few can offer explanation or diagnosis.

Like the Iraqi attack, the psychological abuse and impact, rather than the direct, physical abuse and impact of religious trauma, claims the most victims. But very often, these victims don't even know that they're victims—most have no idea that the name for what they have experienced is "trauma". This is largely because of the dismissive and dangerous feedback loop in which the authoritarian power structure has them entrapped, but also because the (albeit justified) focus on extreme cases of physical and sexual abuse from religious systems prevents survivors from recognizing and validating their own psychological abuse. Yet their bodies learn from the stories, read from the scripts, enact the roles, and perpetuate cycles of fear that manifest in a range of psychological and physical imbalance, and often even sickness and disease.

As Peter Levine points out, the bottom line regarding trauma is what has registered as traumatic to an organism is in their individual felt sense (Levine 132). People who spent their formative and developmental years reacting with fear to the teachings of Evangelicalism were conditioned to dissociate from their bodies in order to become "holy". Individuals who have been repeatedly traumatized as young children often adopt dissociation as a preferred mode of being in the world (Levine 138). We need to extend our previously conceived notion that only physical abuse is traumatizing for a child. Certain patterns of thought, or fixation on an imagined reality, can be equally traumatizing if there is no opportunity for release or resolution of safety.

The emerging field of psychoneuroimmunology teaches us that chronic psychological stress has the power to create physiological changes and effect consequences within the human body. This field of study connects the immune system and the brain and reveals that a trauma response affects not only the immediate bodily functions, but long-term health. People raised under Evangelical doctrines are forced to wage war with their flesh, and their personalities, in order to be considered holy. It shouldn't be a stretch to see that living under such chronic stress is likely to suppress immunological responses. I spent decades singing songs and repeating prayers about the sinful state of the body and my experience is not unique. A quick search on the internet finds

"Powerful prayers of Warfare applying the Blood of Jesus for Protection" (Fernandes), and prayers like "Save me from that Unclean Spirit, Wash me in the Precious Blood to make me White as Snow" (Rampersad).

Research indicates that significant stress can arise from merely thinking about something unpleasant in commonplace experiences, such as taking a test (Martin 88). This particular example stands out to me, as the experience of taking and passing a test is so related to the measure of personal worth and approval from those in authority. In Evangelical circles, perfection is demanded—yet not attained—daily causing inner conflict and fracturing self-worth. And as Dr. Bessel van der Kolk writes, "Suppressing our inner cries for help does not stop our stress hormones from mobilizing the body" (van der Kolk 99). Rather, these cries manifest as physical symptoms that demand our attention in order to heal.

Knowing my own experience and the experiences others have shared with me, I am easily able to equate the example of exam stress with the performance stress of appearing holy within my former Evangelical religious environment. And while it is true that genetic factors may predispose an individual to specific imbalances and illnesses, it is often environmental factors that trigger the full development and expression of many conditions. The brain and immune system are deeply connected to one another by nerve connections, and the tissues of the immune system are bound to the central nervous system—

or as Dr. Martin would say, "The brain and the immune system speak the same languages" (Martin 90). There is an inextricable link between how we feel about ourselves and how we actually, physically feel.

Evangelicalism "diagnoses" a specific sickness for which it claims to have the sole cure, and this is how the power structure of religious belief maintains psychological and physiological control over individuals. And while I am not suggesting that the dismantling of Evangelical Christianity and its traumatizing language will eradicate the genetic predispositions for certain physical imbalances, I am suggesting that the removal of this damaging language—and the power structure responsible for it—could remove systemic triggers that contribute to the development and expression of such conditions and diseases. When environmental triggers that are preventing an individual from feeling safe in their own bodies are removed from a person's experiential reality, they can begin to connect with themselves and heal.

Recently, in a session with a client, I asked her what the moment was that connected her with what had happened to her in a way that allowed her to call it "trauma". She told me that it was the moment she heard elements of her own experience in someone else's story. That experience acted as a mirror to her and gave her language she hadn't had access to before. At that moment she simultaneously realized she was allowed to call what she had experienced "trauma", and that she needed to recover. The validation of her experience extended an invitation to her to begin her journey of healing.

All over the world, people are now waking up to the true reality of their experiences within Evangelicalism because they're hearing their own story inside of someone else's. They're sharing freely and openly, and finding support that allows them to connect with their deep need for healing. The process is easier and faster for some, and it is longer and more difficult for others. But for every person on their own unique path towards recovery, there has to be a moment when they know they can begin. Every person needs to finally the feel permission to call what happened to them by its true name—religious trauma.

In a particularly notable excerpt from *Leaving the Fold*, Winell quotes a woman recovering from her experience with fundamentalist belief who says, "My friend said that when she first left, all she knew was that her favorite color was pink and what her name was. She is fine now, and I will be too" (Winell 11). Long before I came across these two sentences, I had been telling my own story and describing the form of my disconnection from myself by saying that when I left Evangelicalism, I didn't even know my favorite color. That was how separated and disconnected from myself I had become over all of those years surviving in that belief system. It wasn't until I had spent a few years outside that I was able to make that simple decision for myself and connect with the inner permission to make such a seemingly innocuous choice.

While this might seem a benign point to anyone who hasn't spent any time in a fundamentalist or authoritarian environment—or especially, experienced it throughout their formative and developmental years—in truth, it speaks volumes. During my time in Evangelical Christianity, specific pleasures and expressions of personal desires were discouraged. The only thing the woman in Winell's work knew was her favorite color. I didn't even know that much because I never felt permitted to experiment with what brought me pleasure enough to decide on what a favorite color could even be.

I remember an exercise that was conducted in my charismatic Evangelical ministry school years ago where my small group leader encouraged us to sit and write out a list of all of the things that brought us joy. The implication was that the things and places and experiences we had decided we loved were the gifts that god had given to us out of his kindness for us to enjoy unto his glory. I sat and stared at a blank page for almost an entire hour—unable to think of a single thing to write down that brought me pleasure and joy. I couldn't think of one thing that I truly loved because I didn't have any external influence, in that exact moment, telling me whether or not each thing I could write down was something I actually had the permission to love. Because of all of the years

I had been required to disconnect from any and all internal influence or my own inner voice, I found myself in a place in my mid-twenties where I didn't have even one answer for what I uniquely loved, what I wanted, or what brought me joy. I had no connection to or relationship with my own inner compass for simple desire, or for un-influenced, embodied pleasure.

It should come as no surprise that this was the same time period when I was routinely self-harming through eating habits, afraid to get a decently paid job because I feared it would indicate that I was selfish or greedy, and whirling around in a cycle of shame regarding my sexuality. I was barely functioning. Riddled with anxiety and depression, I had no capacity for resolution, stillness, or calm within myself. I had no permission for pleasure or knowledge about my own inner world. I had been in a lengthy holding pattern, waiting upon external "divine" influence to move me in one direction or another and to tell me what I could be free to enjoy and love.

My healing journey from that moment to this one was long—it got worse before it got better. I hit multiple rock bottoms, developed imprisoning compulsive behaviors and codependent patterns, and struggled with self-harm, but eventually left organized religion altogether and began rebuilding slowly. For years it was one step forward and two steps back, but gradually, the inner voice of my own Body, my own intuition, my own Divine Being became louder. As my relationship with my true self strengthened, I heard Her more clearly, trusted Her more deeply, and followed Her more confidently in all things; and over time, I came to realize it had been Her voice— not the voice of an external deity—that I had heard all along.

RECOVERY

Marlene Winell outlines the recovery phases for those healing from Religious Trauma Syndrome as separation, confusion, avoidance, feeling, and rebuilding (Winell 16). This list mirrors Peter Levine's outline for healing from other forms of trauma:

Leaving the environment, establishing safety, and releasing emotions. For many coming out of Evangelicalism, leaving the environment and establishing safety spans the separation, confusion, and avoidance phases before arriving at feeling—or releasing emotions—and rebuilding. The initial separation phase looks different for everyone, but to paraphrase what Richard Rohr refers to as catalysts for all enlightenment, separation almost always comes on the heels or either great love or great suffering (Rohr, Daily Meditations). Just as many of the people I work and talk with left because they fell in love with someone who didn't share their beliefs, or moved next door to someone who challenged their worldview of the "other", others share my experience of leaving because of some kind of deep pain.

Many members of the LGBTQ community, people of color, and women who had never felt entirely safe or welcome to be entirely themselves inside white

Evangelicalism arrived at moments when they finally connected with their deep suffering and knew they could no longer stay. People like me who experienced community betrayal and rejection found the emotional toll manifesting in gastrointestinal issues, insomnia, chronic fatigue, chronic pain, suppressed immune system, and panic attacks. When I returned to the United States after my experience on staff at what I would later discover was an Evangelical Christian cult in England, my body went through months of pain and imbalance that eventually resulted in repeated panic attacks every single time I stepped foot inside of a house of worship.

After a few months of suffering through repeated attempts to attend services, I arrived at a place within myself where I couldn't help but get the message. I had to stop going to church. I knew I was not okay, my body was not okay, and I needed to figure out what had happened. So for the first time since the day my seven year old self prayed the salvation prayer in my pastor's office, I allowed myself to prioritize my own needs over the social and cultural expectations placed upon me by the religious community I was a part of. It was the first time I gave myself permission to leave because I knew I had to take care of myself. I gave myself permission to find the peace to stop going, stop trying, stop hopping from one expression to another in an effort to make pieces fit that were simply refusing to do so. I gave myself the permission to stop chasing the shadows of feelings I had been blindly running after for so long, desperately trying to convince myself that I could actually feel. I gave myself permission to engage with doubt and the questions, and to acknowledge that the certainty I had longed for had never once arrived—not in bad times nor good ones, not in the moments of connection or of loss, not in this country or any other, not on a stage, not in a crowd, not on the streets, not knocking on the door of a stranger. The peace, certainty, and assurance I had spent so long waiting for had never truly arrived.

I stopped showing up and pretending in order to give myself some space to figure out what was going on and to try to begin to heal. After only a few short weeks, I realized that I had been waiting for that permission to leave for two decades. It took significant trauma—my body expressing things that my mind and spirit couldn't understand—for me to finally do what I needed to do and to give myself what I actually wanted for the very first time. It was my body reacting the way She reacted, getting my attention through the anxiety, the depression, the compulsive patterns, that finally woke me up. At the end of my rope, my own body's communication with me saved me; my own body's signals sent to me by way of physical imbalance are what rescued me.

Once I finally left the influence of Evangelicalism, I began to hear my own inner voice again—in ways I hadn't been able to since I was a child, since before I had been required to call Her voice the voice of the spirit of an angry, male god. Once I left, I had the permission and the ability to begin to reintegrate those previously separate parts of myself back into one whole identity, and that was the beginning of the end of my religious belief. It was incredibly painful. I lost almost all of my closest relationships, my social structure, my meaning-making mechanisms, my sense of purpose both temporal and eternal, and lost all sense of direction and desire for work in this world as the only skills I had at the time were ministry-based assets. I had to completely start over—as an adult, I had to learn how to make friends, to make independent decisions, assert my individual identity, find hobbies and interests, experience shame-free sexual exploration, reorient myself towards pleasure and desire, and discover my true self for the very first time. I began asking myself hard questions about what I wanted for my life and enrolled in a coaching certification program, which in turn led me to my professional and academic work and gave me an integrated and whole sense of purpose in this world for the first time—helping other individuals recover from their own religious trauma and abuse.

I began to study myself—what had happened to me and to my mind as a result of being raised, believing the things I had to claim to believe, and why it was that I could never really own them. I learned more about the fundamental teachings of Evangelicalism and how they crumbled in the light of logic, reason, history, and science. I began to discover that they were not as infallible as I had previously been taught, not as eternal and not as immutable. I found ways to connect with others who had gone through similar faith deconstructions and felt they had lost everything in experiencing the pain of the loss of who god had been to them. It was then that I discovered the terminology and study of Religious Trauma Syndrome itself and began to understand the true nature of what I had been through and how I needed to heal from it. That led me to unearth the desire to help others understand, help others heal, and bring all of humanity to a point where we are no longer passing down dangerous and traumatic religious doctrine to future generations, but instead are encouraging science, skepticism, and an informed and integrated spirituality while celebrating our humanity and our bodies.

Everything changed when I gave myself the permission to trust myself, to know myself, to connect with myself and that process led me to a wholeness and a healing I never could have dreamed of—and that Evangelicalism never could have offered me. I have begun the long and joyful journey of establishing my relationship towards pleasure, desire, and longing in my own body. I have learned to celebrate my sexuality, my identity as a woman, my female body, and all of my individual and specific personality nuances involved in being the strong woman I have always been. Finally feeling fulfilled, happy, and free inside my own body and mind gave me the courage to leave behind my toxic and abusive relationship with religion, and caused me to decide to pursue trauma therapy in order to heal from those past messages. Ultimately, it was in leaving all of the other stories I had been told about myself and who I was that gave me the permission to begin to write my own story.

The separation phase of leaving my previous environment broke my heart; but that breaking is necessary for an individual to be able connect with what allows them to begin to rebuild. Confusion and avoidance can be a dance, more circular than linear, and the process takes the time it needs. Having patience for oneself during the process is crucial, considering that all notions of personhood, purpose, "relationship to others, explanations about the world, interpretations of the past, expectations for the future, and directions about how to feel, think, make decisions, and lead your life have been lost" (Winell 17). The confusion phase often sets in very quickly because the previously provided foundation of certainty to stand upon is suddenly gone, and avoidance often enters not long after because the overwhelming reality of everything that has been lost or has changed can be too much to handle.

Without support, it can be extremely difficult to move toward connecting with emotions because the former shaming voices of indoctrination haunt, whispering that emotions are sinful. When someone has been taught for so long to dismiss or avoid their own inner world, learning to embrace those emotions is a crucial component of the path to healing, and very often the first step is to give voice and permission for grief. Accessing grief is crucial to any and every healing process, but it can be extremely difficult to do. Connecting with grief is important because it is a sign that an experience has finally moved into the past—which is an indicator that the trauma cycle that a person experiencing PTSD has been stuck inside has now been completed (Rothschild 63).

Giving the self permission to grieve can be especially difficult for people leaving spiritually traumatic environments, as many people don't know that their former believing life is something to emotionally grieve at all, rather than simply something to change their conscious mind about. Some people may even feel silly actively grieving over a god or an idea of god that they no longer actively believe in. The longer someone spends away from their former worldview, the more difficult it can be for them to connect with their own grief and loss from leaving, but without it—true healing, forward motion, and rebuilding cannot happen.

Very often, the sensations that accompany grief are anxiety and fear (Winell 21). Fear of hell, the rapture and the "end times", or deep body memory of perfectionism and anxiety can reawaken, even after the fear of these things have been rejected intellectually. Guilt, as well, is often an ongoing issue and can be extremely difficult to shake. The body remembers trained reactions and postures concerning behavior and thoughts they previously believed to be sinful—even though there is no longer any logical need for repentance and shame. This creates a mind/ body inner reality conflict. There is often no recognition or language for it, no awareness of the split itself or the widening gap over time, and those in recovery can develop frustration with themselves for not being "over it" yet in terms of how paralyzed they continue to be in relationship to their own guilt complex. A common anecdote I hear from my clients regarding their process of recovery from religious trauma is, "I know 'x' is true, but I still feel 'y'".

Leaving a former authoritarian faith system can feel like a divorce and a death at the same time—which makes it not only an extremely complicated form of grief, but with less readily available assistance and no individual person to point to as the source of the pain. Many people haven't been given the opportunity or education to know that their psychological and physiological symptoms may be linked to their former manner of thinking and believing. The further away people get from believing specific Evangelical teachings, the more ridiculous those ideas seem to them, but this can be problematic because it often results in a person putting more pressure on themselves to move on and no longer be affected by it. This can result in people not connecting with their bodies enough to realize that simply because their brains have dismissed teachings and ideas, doesn't mean their bodies don't still need to heal from the physiological trauma brought on by those ideas.

What can be difficult as well for those who have left Evangelicalism and are seeking support is the lack of helping professions that understand the specificity of the Evangelical experience and language. Religious and secular therapists alike may not understand the true severity of the belief experience, and could potentially do more harm than good by either dismissing their trauma or encouraging their client back to a place of belief. Therapists with no religious background may be quick to dismiss the deeply traumatic nature of Evangelical teachings because they don't seem problematic or extreme enough and a client can feel invalidated or unheard. Religious counselors can often either intentionally or accidentally impose the worldview they hold onto their clients who are actively attempting to recover from it, and the client can feel unsafe or manipulated. Individuals desperate for recovery assistance can find it extremely difficult to find healers who understand the nuance of this particular damage.

Another essential part of the recovery process is anger—in fact, it almost always comes before and ushers in the grief so desperately needed to complete the cycle of trauma. Something cannot be mourned unless its existence has been acknowledged, and for many people, their anger signals that acknowledgement. Most people recovering from Evangelicalism wonder what to do with their anger when it starts to arise, and many are often too afraid to engage it and exhaust themselves trying to avoid or disconnect from it. This is because many of them have been previously taught that the acceptable response to upsetting circumstances is immediate forgiveness and forgetting and therefore can't give themselves permission to validate their own feelings as indications of the wrong done to them.

Authoritarian systems train people to believe that their anger is immoral rather than transformative. But anger is an indicator of injustice and owning, allowing, and directing anger is necessary reclamation work—first personally and then collectively. Since anger often serves as the gateway to grief, and grief is the indicator that an event or experience has been relegated to the past, very often for people to begin to heal they need permission to connect fully with their own anger first. This is not an easy task for people who have spent most of their life being told that anger was disobedience and that disobedience was sin. It is vitally important for people recovering from religious trauma to find safe spaces—both therapeutic and communal—that allow for expressions of anger so that the survivor can discharge the energy that they couldn't discharge during their prolonged threat experience.

What so many people who are trying to heal need to know is that there can be safety and acceptance on the other side of expressions of anger so that they can learn how to self-regulate their emotions for potentially the first time. They need to know that it can be safe to express their feelings, even—and often especially—the heavier ones and that those feelings won't overwhelm them or cause them to lose relationship with their community or loved ones. They need to know their bodies need their permission to be angry in order to begin to heal. After spending so many years sweeping away or invalidating emotional realities, recovery from Evangelical belief for many hinges upon being able to advocate for themselves; very often that means finally getting angry about what happened to them.

REBUILDING

After deconstruction, anger, and grief comes reconstruction—in whatever form the individual decides they need. For many people, the rebuilding stage of their recovery and healing sometimes involves discovering their own autonomous identity and self-worth for the first time. People begin to learn how to make decisions for themselves that are rooted in curiosity rather than control, and as they rebuild their sense of self they begin to become more grounded in who they are. The recovery of individuality and personhood is crucial to healing from trauma and developing a sense of internal safety and taking charge of one's own life is pivotal to their recovery from religious trauma in particular (Winell 22.)

Within fundamentalism, humans are trained towards passivity and codependence because of the emphasis put upon external guidance and divine control. The only capability or strength they could hope to have were given to them from outside of themselves; this often serves to bolster patterns of codependency because they still have a residual tendency to look outside themselves for security and satisfaction. This, in turn, can result in addictive tendencies and often leads to codependency in romantic relationships—especially for Evangelical Christian women who have had the learned-helplessness of sub-missive and subservient roles instilled into them for so long. Under Evangelicalism, women who express inde-pendence or autonomy are thought to be disobedient. They're conditioned to aspire to be mothers and wives and discouraged from developing certain necessary life skills because of the expectation that their husbands will handle the majority of the necessary financial and practi-cal tasks for their family.

Critical to recovery for all genders, however, is discov-ering and learning to use their own inner resources. This may sound simple, but it is an incredibly difficult shift for people who have been taught that they either do not have any inner resources or that relying upon the ones they do have is sinful. For recovering Evangelicals, learn-ing how to trust themselves for the very first time can be a difficult journey, as many are getting in touch with the feelings, emotions, and sensations that live within their bodies for the very first time. This begins with each indi-vidual going down a path of steadily releasing permission to themselves to reclaim their right to feel what they feel. To grow and flourish outside of an authoritarian religious construct, every person must know that they are allowed to connect with and understand their emotions, and that their intuition is a valid inner resources that make them fully human and healthy.

When I was on my way out of my own experience with Evangelicalism, I audited a course online with UC Berkeley called the Science of Happiness because I had no idea how to find joy, satisfaction, or happiness within myself on my own—that is how carved out and empty of valid, real, human emotional experience I was. I was in my mid-twenties and I truly did not know how to feel my own feelings—I was numb every moment of every day—and I honestly felt that I needed some tangible and scientific proof that I would be able to be happy on my own at some point. What is ironic to me now is how that behavior speaks to my former fundamentalist scrupulosity—I went straight to data for assistance. When I look back on my notes from that course and my journals from that time, I must sadly acknowledge what was happening in the inner world of that woman: I couldn't feel anything, and I needed empirical evidence to tell me how I might be able to find a way to do so.

What I know now is that I was trying to begin developing my own, autonomous approach to life—which is another thing that every recovering person needs (Winell 23). People must be able to reconstruct their own pattern of meaning, regardless of what it looks like or how long it takes—it simply must be all their own. Experiencing depression or numbness is normal during this phase of recovery (Winell 23). I have had clients who have even gone so far as to describe it by saying, "I don't feel alive." Losing a former faith story means losing the meaning-making method by which a person made sense of their life and the world around them. For former Evangelicals, the primary difficulty is the struggle to consider what it would be like to have an authentic and healthy spirituality, as they are fearful of getting trapped in an alternative authoritarian environment (Winell 23). It is impossible to live without any meaning, structure, story, or purpose, however, and so it is vitally important to allow this part to heal slowly over time.

So how do people on the path to healing and freedom reclaim their feelings, release their emotions, discover an authentic spirituality, and connect with their inner world after being told for so long that all of those things were either off limits or not possible? One—if not the most important—way is by seeking communal and/ or professional support: spaces, places, and relationships that help to establish a sense of personal safety and belonging. This looks different for everyone, as people have varying needs because everyone's body internalizes traumatic experiences in different ways. It may mean engaging with various trauma healing modalities with a professional. It could be somatic techniques for some, mindfulness exercises for others, physical healing for someone else, or even a combination of them all. It could also simply mean locating a community of people who have been through the same experience.

The good news is that our brains are elastic. Our minds can experience healing by exchanging stories and over time our bodies follow suit. Our physical bodies may need some extra care and attention because the deeper somatic memories stored during experiences of trauma can surface by way of unexpected triggers. There are so many avenues and options for healing, many of which I have personally benefited from, and some I even offer to others now.

Breaking free is only half the battle. It was only after I had begun processing through the trauma of my Evangelical experience and started releasing it that I was capable of trading it for a new story. The way I have described my own therapeutic experience was as if the train tracks of my brain rerouted, and I could literally feel that they would never go back. I have a practitioner friend who says that trauma therapy is all about "unlearning"—it isn't easy, and it doesn't happen overnight. If something took you years to learn, it may take years to unlearn it—but as a society, we are arriving at avenues and pathways for physical, mental, and spiritual healing like never before.

Across the board, the primary component that I see as necessary in people healing from Evangelical Christianity is awareness of embodiment. Becoming aware of the body via one method or another is extremely important for establishing a healthy sense of self. There are a number of different techniques and therapeutic methods for increasing body awareness and a felt sense of safety such as massage therapy, myofascial release, somatic body-work, yoga, breathwork, meditation, and energetic medicine. Additionally, touch-based trauma processing therapies such as EMDR and EFT allow the patient to remain in their body and the present moment while accessing and working through former experiences of trauma and these modalities overwhelmingly prove to be more even more effective than medication alone (van der Kolk 256).

As an embodiment coach who helps people through the recovery process of leaving Evangelicalism, I often find anger is the very first emotional gateway to all other emotions and to honest processing of an experience. Somatic and therapeutic approaches that provide a safe, non-judgmental space and support clients in giving themselves permission to fully feel and process emotion are deeply integral to the healing process. In a very real sense, the reorientation towards pleasure involves the validation of experienced pain. The suppression of heavy emotions limits the human capacity to feel more positive ones like pleasure and delight within the body as well.

In order to rebuild from the trauma of Evangelical belief, an individual must establish a relationship with their body, intuition, and personal agency. Without a solid connection to their deepest and truest self, people run the risk of being pulled into another authoritarian influence or form of fundamentalism. In my work as a coach, I use storytelling as a healing modality. It's vitally important for people recovering to own their own voice and story, to do the necessary inner investigative work to notice and name their issues, to be empowered to speak kindly to and heal themselves, and to become aware of the relationship they are in with themselves after years of coerced neglect of self.

Storytelling as a healing modality is a core component of narrative therapy and narrative medicine, and has its roots in the healing power of expression. I believe the need to share stories drives many people to seek out communities and individuals to be honest and share their experiences with. Those relationships and communal spaces can simulate their former experience of congregational gathering and belonging that is often sorely missed after leaving Evangelical environments. The difference in these new chosen families, however, is that within them there is a new sense of safety when self-actualization needs are included and validated by the community. Opening up, telling their story, and taking ownership back over their own personal narrative is crucial to survivors' ability to release the body's accumulated stress of traumatizing environments and helps the body begin to release chronic stress-related physical imbalances.

Narrative medicine has recorded examples of chronic conditions, including autoimmune diseases, leaving the body of a person who becomes reconciled to themselves after traumatizing experiences. Lewis Mehl-Madrona tells a compelling story of his work with a woman raised as an Evangelical Christian who had spent many years as a dutiful and submissive wife and mother before she developed the autoimmune disease lupus. The crucial detail that stuck out to me is that through her treatment with Mehl-Madrona, and after owning her own story by writing, she eventually developed the practice of simply telling her body that she did not need the lupus anymore. The story she had decided upon for her own healing was that she was able to thank her illness and invite it to leave because it had accomplished its work of sending her the messages she needed to learn about leaving her religion, her marriage, and her formerly submissive identity (Mehl-Madrona 25). At the time of Mehl-Madrona's retelling of her experience, this woman had been completely free and healed of lupus for twenty years.

I have seen similar breakthroughs in the pacification or full healing of physical conditions in my work with my own clients. Once the body feels and knows it is being heard, understood, and related to kindly, the body can begin to feel safe to heal. I have had clients with chronic illness see their symptoms reverse and not develop into full-blown autoimmune disease, clients with cancer see it disappear and those with reproductive issues conceive naturally. I've seen healing in physical limitations in their sexual dysfunction and many free themselves from formerly imprisoning dissociative patterns by way of writing letters, books, plays, poetry, and music that facilitates their ability to hear the voice of their body. In writing and creating, they have validated their anger, their sadness, and the full range of their emotional experience of what happened to them that was received within their body as abuse.

Story-based intuitive embodiment work allows a sense of safety and trust to be established in the physical body—the very body that many of the people I work with were told for decades was untrustworthy, deceitful, wicked, evil, and deserving of pain. For many, this relational reconnection with themselves is a brand new experience of learning to trust and be connected with their body for the very first time. It speaks to the necessary unlearning process for many coming out of Evangelical environments because for so long the physical body was seen as something dangerous or guilty or of providing, at the least, false information about reality and, at the worst, a reason for eternal torture.

If it is true that emotional expression has healing properties for the human immune system, then we know that the suppression of emotions is damaging to immune system. Interestingly, allopathic medicine doesn't claim to know where or how autoimmune conditions originate, but attempted explanations often involve the immune system receiving a message that a certain part of the body was its own enemy. That language is frightening similar to the language Evangelicalism uses to claim that the physical body is filled with sin and should not be considered a part of what is holy about a person. The further away from the ability to receive and recognize the body's signals of a desire to seek safety, the wider that gap of dissociation becomes and the sicker a person can become.

Unfortunately, the Evangelical narrative has its own answer for where illness and pain comes from—either attacks from evil forces attempting to get you to stop placing your trust in god or spiritual tests of devotion from this supposed loving god. This mindset creates a dangerous feedback loop of further body dissociation and keeps people sick, weak, susceptible, and needing more of what the authoritarian answer is claiming to offer. Believing these notions further separates someone from the ability to be in communication with their body and to register physical symptoms as messengers from within attempting to communicate inner-imbalance and internalized trauma.

As Peter Levine says, "Until we understand that traumatic symptoms are physiological as well as psychological, we will be woefully inadequate in our attempts to heal them (Levine 32). This idea is what the innate healing capacity of storytelling for healing hinges upon—it allows a person to wrestle with and discover the meaning of their symptoms in light of their experiences. The narrative approach to healing states that in order to heal, an individual has to figure out where their imbalance or condition came from, what message it is trying to send them, and what it is trying to communicate to them about what they have too much of, or what they're lacking. Until the pain or condition within a person's body no longer conveys an unresolved issue, it will continue to be recycled into their being to protect the traumatized individual in situations of potential threat and arousal (Scaer 104).

Our ability to create fiction, retell the past, and speak of potential futures is what allowed us as homosapiens to develop into our species in the first place, and it is that very ability that is at the root of our propensity towards belief and religion (Harari 25). Because of this, our immune systems are more vulnerable to psychological and emotional influences than those of species who lack the ability to move between past, present, and future (Martin 90). There is the potential, then, that mindfulness and consciousness practices such as yoga and meditation can lead those who have been negatively or traumatically affected by a constant state of fear and worry toward future health. Not surprising, I suppose, when we remember that the true roots of Christianity—the teachings of Jesus the Christ—are not so different from spiritual traditions such as Buddhism.

If a person is able to dismantle their former religious dogma by recognizing its fallacy, understanding and validating the way they have been harmed, and growing into the self-permission to feel safe without it, they can experience release from the grips of the twisted moral codes previously imposed upon them. Practitioners, friends, family, and communities who can provide recovering people with the access, information and opportunity to set themselves free from these abusive religious narratives can help them enter into a safe and sacred space within themselves from which to explore and delight in their own humanity. And, in the same way that it is necessary for an individual to release themselves from abusive doctrines such as hell and sin nature, it is vital for every healed person to offer access, information, and opportunity to others to learn how—and to what extent—the Evangelical paradigm is causing harm to psychological states, physical bodies, and spiritual expressions.

So much of the work of healing hinges on the practice of embodiment, and so much of that practice hinges upon increased personal awareness. It all starts in simply beginning to notice. This is underlined when my clients tell stories of former manners of behaving, living, and moving that had been their normal until the moment they noticed for the very first time that they had been doing something or responding in a way that had been harmful all along. In my work, I call those sudden revelatory moments invitations unto bearing non-judgmental witness to oneself—there is no need to rush to try and change what has been brought to the surface. Noticing is the first step out of the cycle of dissociation. The development of dual consciousness, or noticing what is happening within and experiencing what is happening without, is crucial for healing and re-association to the body.

When a young tree is injured, it grows around its injury (Levine 33). That's the rub about wild and living things—they respond to their environments honestly. Our bodies are alive and wild and honest and the ways they grow so tenaciously around the wounds of the pasts is the rhythm of nature, a thing of great beauty. In the internal and external symptoms of trauma are the very energies, potentials, and resources necessary for their healing and transformation (Levine 37). People coming out of the authoritative and traumatic religious construct of Evangelicalism need to honor their resistance, remember that a new life is possible, and just keep trying. Learning an entirely new manner of living and moving in the world is like building a new habit slowly, or exercising a muscle that has atrophied while compassionately recognizing that the atrophy may have been the body believing it was saving a life. Be patient, be gentle, be kind, and have hope. Our bodies are on our team.

Most importantly, those who have healed from this particular traumatic experience of believing and then leaving Evangelical Christianity are desperately needed to help lead others out. Many who came from positions of pastoring, leading, teaching, and caring often feel aimless without an eternal mission because their felt sense of purpose disappeared along with their former beliefs. But their purpose, their stories, and their meaning can be reborn as a passion for one another—still pastoring, still healing, and still ministering; but for the here and now, for the integration of the whole person.

There is a greater commission to be found in helping to heal the ones who are leaving, while simultaneously working to increase cultural awareness of the harmful nature of Evangelical teachings unto the dismantling of the system for the flourishing of all people. Those whose safety, lovability, and acceptance depended on the good news of Evangelical Christianity need an invitation to their new life on the other side. Once they reconnect to themselves, they will be able to stand firm in the full awareness that all people are safe and loved and accepted just as they are. They can find their purpose in this new and real good news to share: You are your own. Just as you have always been.

CONCLUSION

Throughout my research and lived experience, the most vital component has been recognizing that if something isn't self-critical, it isn't as valuable as it could be. This proved to be difficult to accomplish as I was writing much of this work through the lens of the pain of my personal experience and the experiences of those I hold space for my in professional work. Developing a curiosity about my own biases was quite a stretch, as I had spent so long inside of a paradigm that required absolute certainty. Developing the ability to be self-critical at first felt like I was somehow breaking a rule that my body had been believing She needed to follow in order to survive. It was arduous, but in the end it was a gift—and a skill I want to continue to develop.

In a very real sense, this book itself is my first part of a larger, lifelong work. I want to continue this study of the deep impact of Evangelical purity culture's brand of sexual repression: the psychological and physical impact upon those required to separate themselves from their sexuality and their physical bodies during their development in order to belong. I want to further explore modal-

ities of embodiment for healing through avenues of research, training, and practice. I hope you join me in this
process.

BIBLIOGRAPHY

Cox, D., & Jones, R. P., PhD. (2017, September 6). America's Changing Religious Identity. Retrieved from https://www.prri.org/research/american-religious-landscape-christian-religiously-unaffiliated/

Dolan, E. W. (2015, April 26). Post-traumatic stress disorder can destroy sexual health -- regardless of the type of trauma experienced. Retrieved from https://www.psypost.org/2015/04/post-traumatic-stress-disorder-can-destroy-sexual-health-regardless-of-the-type-of-trauma-experienced-33816

Fernandes, G. (2017, September 25). Powerful prayers of warfare applying the blood of Jesus for protection. Retrieved from https://www.youtube.com/watch?v=WQdXHgMXaTs

Fitzgerald, Frances. *The Evangelicals: The Struggle to Shape America*. New York, NY: Simon & Schuster, 2017.

Gerson, Michael. "The Last Temptation: How Evangelicals, Once Culturally Confident, Became an Anxious Minority Seeking Political Protection from the Least Traditionally Religious President in Living Memory" *The Atlantic*, April 2018. Retrieved from: https://www.theatlantic.com/magazine/archive/2018/04/the-last-temptation/554066/

Gushee, David P. *Still Christian: Following Jesus out of American Evangelicalism*. Louisville, KY: Westminster John Knox Press, 2017.

Harari, Yuval N. *Sapiens: A Brief History of Humankind*. New York, NY: Harper, 2015.

Herman, Judith Lewis. *Trauma and Recovery*. New York: BasicBooks, 1997.

Jenkins, C., & Garcia-Navarro, L. (2018, November 11). The American Academy Of Pediatrics On Spanking Children: Don't Do It, Ever. Retrieved from https://www.npr.org/2018/11/11/666646403/ the-american-academy-of-pediatrics-on-spanking-children-dont-do-it-ever?utm_source=facebook. com&utm_medium=social&utm_campaign=npr&utm_ term=nprnews&utm_content=2041&fbclid=IwAR0n 8QeURi83vCgisXyPplUhJNvZswkxro7iB6he3HwnTslt 2g-5paHv7EY

Ladd, C. (2018, June 16). The article removed from Forbes, "Why White Evangelicalism Is So Cruel". Retrieved from https://www.politicalorphans. com/the-article-removed-from-forbes-why-white-evangelicalism-is-so-cruel/

Levine, Peter. *Waking the Tiger, Healing Trauma: The Innate Capacity to Transform Overwhelming Experiences*. Berkeley: North Atlantic Books, 1997.

Martin, Paul. *The Healing Mind: The Vital Links Between Brain and Behavior, Immunity and Disease*. New York, NY: St. Martin's Press, 1997.

Mehl-Madrona, Lewis. *Coyote Wisdom: The Power of Story in Healing*. Rochester, VT: Bear & Co., 2005.

Our Denomination. (2018). Retrieved from http://www. faithchurchaustin.org/about/our-denomination

Rampersad, C. (2018, December 06). "Prayer for Purity of Mind, Body and Soul." *TT Christian.* Retrieved from https://christianstt.com/ daily-prayer-purity-mind-body-soul/

Rohr, R. (2013). Richard Rohr's Daily Meditation. Retrieved from https://myemail. constantcontact.com/Richard-Rohr-s-Daily-Meditation--Great-Love-and-Great-Suffering. html?soid=1103098668616&aid=kIg8_QJ8oEQ

Rothschild, Babette. *The Body Remembers: The Psychophysiology of Trauma and Trauma Treatment.* New York: Norton, 2000.

Scaer, Robert C. *The Body Bears the Burden: Trauma, Dissociation, and Disease.* New York: Haworth Medical Press, 2001.

Stroop, Chrissy. (2017, September 03). "Break the Cycle: Spiritual Abuse and the Conversion of Children." *Unfundamentalist Parenting.* Retrieved from https://www.patheos.com/ blogs/unfundamentalistparenting/2017/09/ break-cycle-spiritual-abuse-conversion-children/

Van Der Kolk, M.D., Bessel. *The Body Keeps the Score: Brain, Mind, and Body in the Healing of Trauma.* 375 Hudson St., New York, NY 10014: Penguin Group, 2014.

Watters, Wendell. *Deadly Doctrine: Health, Illness, and Christian God-Talk.* Amherst, New York: Prometheus Books, 1992.

Wilbanks, Jessica. *When I Spoke in Tongues: A Story of Faith and Its Loss*. Boston, MA: Beacon Press, 2018.

Winell, Marlene. *Leaving the Fold: A Guide for Former Fundamentalists and Others Leaving Their Religion*. Oakland, CA: New Harbinger Publications, 1993.

Winell, Marlene. (2016, July 13). "Religious Trauma Syndrome." *Journey Free: Recovery from Harmful Religion.* Retrieved from https://journeyfree.org/rts/

Wormald, B. (2017, September 07). "America's Changing Religious Landscape." Retrieved from http://www.pewforum.org/2015/05/12/americas-changing-religious-landscape/

ACKNOWLEDGEMENTS

Strange as it may sound, I would have never finished this book without Twitter.

Thank you to the chorus of voices that I've found in that bizarre little corner of the internet who offered me the perfect encouragement in some of my harder and heavier moments. You honestly deserve as much credit as my therapist.

Thank you also to my real life friends and chosen family whose real life words also saved me and shoved me forward at the most pivotal moments: my academic advisors Karen Campbell and Francis Charet; my therapist Alan Pennington; my partner Todd Burman; my family: Jim Finch, Jake Fuchs and Angie Collier, Joyce and Joe Rees; my many, many dearest ones (including but not limited to) Chandra Fredrickson, Hayley Hayes, Emilia Paré, Hillary McBride, Audrey Assad, Emily Blincoe, Elle Malmstrom, William Matthews, Corey Pigg, Dru Parrish, Kevin Garcia, Arden Leigh, Corey Pigg, Kendal Hillman, Alexis Viele, Shannon Douglas, #LasLobas, and the #cuntcoven; my Airing of Grief team—Jon Allen, Kevin MacDougall, and Derek Webb; Caitlin Metz for her brilliant artistic design and ever-compassionate timeline; Tucker FitzGerald for his generous assistance in getting this work into print; Corinne Cordasco and Melissa Montecuollo for their editing expertise; my brave and incredible clients who teach me and heal me everyday; and all of the podcast communities who first gave me their platforms to talk about this work that I care about more than anything in the whole world—The Life After, The Liturgists, Exvangelical, Millenneagram, Out of Line, The Twisted Sisterds, and The Inglorious Pasterds.

And last but never, ever least: Thank you to my Body for loving me and saving my life.

-Jamie

ABOUT JAMIE

Jamie Lee Finch is a sexuality and embodiment coach, intuitive healer, self-conversation facilitator, sex witch, and poet. She believes our bodies have a language and that language is our mother tongue. Trauma in any form—including toxic experiences with authoritarian religious belief—is responsible for breaking down our ability to communicate successfully with our bodies; and any sort of illness or imbalance, dysfunction or disease is our bodies' frustrated but loving attempt to reconnect with and communicate to us. The work that she does is in reassociating people with their bodies, the language their body is speaking, and the voice their body is speaking with; it is deep reconciliation healing work on a mental, emotional, spiritual, and physical level.

You can learn about Jamie's work at JamieLeeFinch.com.

Made in the USA
Coppell, TX
26 January 2021